Seniors

Guide to
Alexa

Welcome

What's the first thing that comes to mind when you think of Alexa? It's probably a smart speaker that answers questions and performs basic tasks. It turns out, however, that Alexa is so much more than that. Not only is it a personal assistant, but it can also make phone and video calls, order products from Amazon, stream movies and TV shows, and even entertain your dog.

It also comes in many shapes and sizes, from a small puck that you can tuck away in a corner to a massive 10-inch touchscreen that can automatically swivel its screen to follow you around the room. In short, Alexa is an ever-expanding service that covers software, hardware, and everything in between.

This book is a guide to everything you need to know about Alexa. You'll learn how Alexa works, the many different devices it supports, how to set up Alexa, talk to it, and use it to improve your life in so many ways. Turn over the page, and you'll find the book contents, which provides a brief glance at what you can expect to find in each chapter. Alternatively, jump to the back of the book to see a more detailed index.

Just before I go, if there's anything you would like to know that isn't covered in this book, send me an email at tom@leafpublishing.co.uk, and I'll be more than happy to help.

Tom Rudderham
Author
tom@leafpublishing.co.uk

Credits:

Author: Tom Rudderham
Editor: Zeljko Jurancevic

Published by:
Leaf Publishing LTD
www.leafpublishing.co.uk

ISBN:
9798516298622

Contents

Welcome

Setting Up

Get to Know Alexa

Music, audiobooks, and video

Communication

Shopping & information

Lists, alerts, and calendar

Skills and routines

Create a smart home

Discover Alexa's funny side

Privacy and security

Troubleshooting

Chapter 01

Welcome

Alexa is unlike any computer you've used before. It comes in many shapes and sizes, from a puck-sized speaker to a large swivelling touchscreen. It's totally hands-free, which means you can use Alexa by simply talking out loud. It's incredibly clever, able to answer nearly any question you can think of. It gets to know you over time by adapting to your speech patterns, vocabulary, and personal preferences. It also has a dry sense of humour. No, really, just ask it to tell a joke.

In this chapter, we'll get to know Alexa. We'll explore how it works, what it can do, check out the types of devices it supports, and help you decide which device is best suited for you (if you haven't already made a decision).

In this chapter:

Get to know Alexa

Meet your virtual assistant...

Think of Alexa as your very own personal assistant. One that's always listening — even from the other side of the room — and ready to respond to your voice commands. In many ways, Alexa is the most natural way to interact with a computer. It's how we as humans have communicated with each other for tens of thousands of years, and while desktop computers have had voice command software for some time, Alexa is the most successful and intuitive voice command system yet. To understand why this is, you need to consider a number of things:

- We all speak with slightly different accents, dialects, and languages. For a voice command system to work successfully, it needs to understand the nuances present across a variety of accents. Unlike the voice command systems you might find on a desktop computer or in your car, Alexa can recognise localised accents across eight languages: English, French, German, Hindi, Italian, Japanese, Portuguese (Brazilian), and Spanish.

- You can ask questions in a massive number of ways, and Alexa will understand. To give an example, if you wanted to find out what the weather is like, you could ask, "Alexa, what's the weather outside?" or "Alexa, is it going to rain today?", or even "Alexa, do I need to take an umbrella?"

- It's always listening. 24 hours a day. It's waiting for the keyword "Alexa" to be spoken out loud. Once this is recognised, Alexa starts listening to your voice while simultaneously sending the data back to Amazon's headquarters. This data is analysed by software to identify command questions and commands, then the answer is sent back to your Alexa device and played back in audio form through the speakers. While this might pose any number of privacy concerns, keep in mind that Alexa only sends data back home after the keyword "Alexa" is triggered. It's not listening to your conversations or recording what you do.

Because Alexa is so good at voice recognition, and so fast at responding, it has quickly become the most successful 'personal assistant' in the world. Once you become familiar with the various Alexa devices, you'll start to see them everywhere, including peoples homes, offices, and even in cars. This may come as a surprise, because unlike traditional voice command software, Alexa doesn't open apps or access menus. Instead, it can do the following:

- Tell you the latest news, weather, or traffic

- Create to-do lists

- Set reminders and alarms

- Play music, podcasts, and audiobooks

- Buy something from Amazon

- Control smart devices, such as lights and door locks

- Tell jokes and entertain pets

That last one might catch you off guard, but it's one of Alexa's most enduring traits: a sense of whimsy and humour. It makes Alexa seem less like a robot and more relatable. Even fun to use once you've learned a few tricks (which we'll get to later in this book).

How Alexa works

The basics of how Alexa turns words into commands...

You might think of Alexa as a single object. Something that listens to your voice and immediately responds, but Alexa is far more complicated than it appears to be. It's actually a collection of services that work over the internet, and when combined, result in a rather magical service that can do thousands of things. These four components are what enables Alexa to work so brilliantly:

Voice recognition

You might think Alexa recognises the words you say out loud, but it can only recognise one word: Alexa. The device you own is constantly listening for this single word, which Amazon calls the wake word.

Voice recording

Once the wake word has been triggered, your Alexa device starts recording your voice using a built-in microphone. It waits until there's a sensible pause, then it sends the voice recording over the internet and back to Amazon's headquarters.

Alexa Voice Service (AVS)

Over at Amazon's HQ, an artificial intelligence called Alexa Voice Service (AVS for short), listens to your voice recording and almost instantly translates it into a set of instructions. These are then converted into a result and sent back across the internet to your Alexa device.

Speech synthesis

The results beamed back from Amazon's AVS are converted into recognisable speech using a set of audio files stored within your Alexa. These are played back through speakers, followed by any relevant services that were requested (such as music playback).

As you might have guessed, Alexa doesn't actually live inside the device you own, but rather in Amazon's HQ — which might be on the opposite side of the planet to where you live. As a result, Alexa is very much an internet-based service, so you'll always need a web connection for it to work.

The basic flow of Alexa

1. **You say "Alexa" out loud.**

Your device wakes up. This is indicated by a chime and (in most cases) a blue ring of light.

2. **You ask a question or a command.**

Alexa records your command. When there's a suitable pause, the recording is sent over the internet to Amazon's AVS.

3. **AVS uses complex speech recognition analysis to turn the recording into keywords.**

Not every word is translated. Only keywords that can be translated into a command.

4. **These keywords are then converted into a command or question.**

If AVS can't fulfil your command directly, then it shares the request with third-party services (such as Wikipedia) and gathers a response.

5. **AVS sends the response back to your local Alexa device.**

Your Alexa plays back the response using audio speakers (plus visual results if you have an Alexa with a screen).

What Alexa can do

Alexa is more than just a smart speaker...

Alexa is far more capable than you might imagine. Behind the scenes, somewhere in northern American, a vast collection of supercomputers (also known as "the cloud") powers Alexa's artificial intelligence. Alexa can answer pretty much any question, control the devices in your home, help you shop, schedule your day, and much more, as we'll explore on these two pages...

Answer questions

Alexa is brilliant at answering your questions. Whatever you can think of, she'll know the answer. Wondering what the weather is going to be like next week? Alexa will know. Want to know how just won the Oscar for best actor? Alexa can tell you. Topics Alexa knows about include trivia, history, weather, facts, traffic conditions, and so much more.

News and information

Alexa is totally up to date on the latest news stories, sports scores, and weather. Every morning you can ask for a Flash Briefing (just say, "Alexa, give me my Flash Briefing"), and you'll get all the latest news in a concise and entertaining manner. You can also customise your Flash Briefing to get updates on local news or from your favourite news station.

Playing music

As soon as you turn on your Echo for the first time, it's ready to start playing music from Amazon Music - an ad-based music service that can play nearly every song, album, and playlist. You can also subscribe to Amazon Music Unlimited to remove ads or connect your Alexa to your favourite music service (such as Apple Music or Spotify). With its multi-room support and punchy speakers, Alexa makes for the perfect way to listen to music, audiobooks, podcasts, or radio stations throughout the house.

Watching video

If you own an Echo device with a screen (such as an Echo Spot or Show), then it's possible to watch your favourite streaming services, such as Amazon Prime or Netflix, on its touchscreen. You can also ask Alexa to play a video from YouTube, Vimeo, or Daily Motion.

Communicating

You wouldn't think of Alexa as a way to chat with friends and family, but that's precisely what you can do. Not only can you make phone calls to other Echo devices (or even mobile phones), but you can send text messages via the Alexa app and make video calls using an Echo Spot or Show. It's also possible to use your Echo devices as a walkie-talkie and talk to people in other rooms.

Being helpful

We all have busy lives, so having a pair of extra hands (even virtual hands) around the house can be helpful. Alexa can make shopping lists for you, set a timer or alarm, and even manage your calendar. Head over to the *Lists, alerts, and calendar* to find out more.

Controlling smart devices

Alexa can control any number of smart devices in your home, such as door locks, lights, thermostats, security cameras, and smart plugs; basically, anything that's controllable over a Wi-Fi connection. To learn more, turn to the *Create a smart home* chapter.

Almost anything else, using *skills*

Alexa is incredibly intelligent straight out of the box, but by adding skills to your device, you can do things like order a takeaway pizza, play quizzes, make a donation, get nutrition tips or receipt ideas, plus much, much more. To find out more about Alexa skills, jump to chapter 08.

Alexa devices

Discover where to find Alexa, and what shapes and forms it comes in...

When you think of Alexa, what's the first image that comes to mind? It might be a small speaker with a fabric covering, or you might imagine a small rectangular block with a screen on the front. In reality, Alexa comes in many shapes and forms, but there are two types of devices:

Official Alexa devices

These are the products you can purchase directly from Amazon. You'll find more details about each over the next few pages. In short there's the Amazon Echo, the Echo Dot, Echo Spot, Echo Show, Echo Studio, Echo Auto, Echo Buds, Echo Flex, and Echo Sub. Amazon is constantly updating and adding new products, which means Alexa becomes more versatile and powerful with each passing month.

Devices that can Alexa can control

One of Alexa's most useful features is the ability to control a large number of third-party devices. There are tens of thousands available to purchase, including smart lights, door locks, security cameras, speakers, smart plugs, and thermostats. To give an example, you could use Alexa to turn the lights on. You can also group lights together, enabling you to turn them all on and off at once, or activate individual groups (such as upstairs and downstairs lights).

Alexa can also control devices indirectly. For example if you have an old fashioned lamp plugged into a smart plug, by using Alexa to turn the plug on and off, you can power the lamp indirectly.

Echo Dot

Think of Alexa, and this is the first product that might come to mind...

This is the most popular Alexa device you can buy. It features a compact globe design that fits perfectly into small spaces, and a single 1.6-inch speaker that's surprisingly loud. It also has a fabric covering that's both durable and easy to clean (helpful if your Alexa is in the kitchen!) An additional version with a built-in LED clock is also available. With the ability to display the current time, it's perfect for bedside tables.

Specifications:

- **Size:** 100 x 100 x 89 mm (3.9" x 3.9" x 3.5")

- **Weight:** 328 grams

- **Wi-Fi:** Dual Band 802.11 a/b/g/n/ac (2.4 and 5 GHz) networks.

- **Audio:** 1.6" speaker

- **Output:** 3.5 mm stereo audio

- **Colours:** Charcoal, Glacier White, Twilight Blue

Echo

A more powerful version of the Dot...

Designed for larger spaces, the Echo delivers clear highs, dynamic mids, and deep bass for rich, detailed sound that fills any room. If you're planning to use Alexa to play music throughout the house, then the Echo is a wonderful option that's both affordable, yet powerful. It also has a temperature sensor, enabling it to both tell you the current conditions in the house, while also accurately controlling smart thermostats.

Specifications:

- **Size:** 144 x 144 x 133 mm (5.0" x 5.0" x 4.7")
- **Weight:** 970 grams
- **Wi-Fi:** Dual-band 802.11 a/b/g/n/ac (2.4 and 5 GHz) networks
- **Audio:** 3" neodymium woofer and 2 x 0.8" tweeters
- **Output:** 3.5 mm stereo audio
- **Colours:** Charcoal, Glacier White, PRODUCT(RED), Twilight Blue

Echo Spot

Combining visual results and video calls with Alexa...

This is the most popular Alexa device you can buy. It features a compact globe design that fits perfectly into small spaces, and a single 1.6-inch speaker that's surprisingly loud. It also has a fabric covering that's both durable and easy to clean (helpful if your Alexa is in the kitchen!) An additional version with a built-in LED clock is also available. With the ability to display the current time, it's perfect for bedside tables.

Specifications:

- **Size:** 104 mm x 97 mm x 91 mm (4.1" x 3.8" x 3.6")
- **Weight:** 420 grams
- **Wi-Fi:** Wi-Fi: Dual-band 802.11 a/b/g/n/ac (2.4 and 5 GHz) networks
- **Audio:** 1.6" speaker
- **Output:** 3.5 mm stereo audio
- **Colours:** Charcoal, Glacier White, PRODUCT(RED), Twilight Blue

Echo Show

An intuitive touchscreen & support for video calls...

With a vibrant 8-inch touchscreen, the Echo Show lets you make video calls, watch TV shows and movies, display music lyrics (UK only at the time of writing), view security cameras around your home, recipe instructions, plus much more. All of this is combined with Alexa's voice results, making the Echo Show the most versatile of the Echo devices, and a great addition to any smart home.

Specifications:

- **Size:** 200.4 x 135.9 x 99.1 mm (7.9" x 5.3" x 3.9")

- **Weight:** 1037 grams

- **Display:** 8" touchscreen

- **Wi-Fi:** Dual-band 802.11 a/b/g/n/ac (2.4 and 5 GHz) networks

- **Audio:** 2" (52 mm) neodymium speakers with passive bass radiator.

- **Colours:** Charcoal fabric, Sandstone fabric

Echo Show 10

The ultimate Alexa experience...

With a huge 10.1-inch touchscreen that swivels during a video to keep you in frame, a 13MP camera, and a range of speakers that can fill a room, the Echo Show 10 is pretty much the ultimate Alexa experience. It's the perfect Echo for your living room, where you can watch a TV show or movie on Amazon Prime on its large display, make video calls with pin-sharp video quality, interact with Alexa using both your voice and your fingertips.

Specifications:

- **Size:** 9.9" x 9" x 6.7" (251 x 230 x 172mm)
- **Weight:** 2560 grams (2.56 kg)
- **Display:** 10.1" swivelling touchscreen
- **Wi-Fi:** Wi-Fi: Dual-band 802.11 a/b/g/n/ac (2.4 and 5 GHz) networks
- **Audio:** 2.1 System: 2 x 1.0" tweeters and a 3.0" woofer
- **Colours:** Charcoal, Glacier White

Echo Studio

Incredible room-filling audio...

With it's five speaker system, the Echo Studio creates an immersive, three-dimensional soundscape, wrapping you in studio-quality audio from every direction. That's thanks to support for Dolby Atmos, which enables a multidimensional audio experience, adding space, clarity and depth. The Echo Studio will also automatically analyse the acoustics of your room, fine-tuning playback for optimal sound, no matter where its placed. If you're looking for the best audio experience available for Alexa, then this is it.

Specifications:

- **Size:** 206 x 175 mm (8.11" x 3.8" x 6.9")

- **Weight:** 3.5 kg

- **Wi-Fi:** Wi-Fi: Dual-band 802.11 a/b/g/n/ac (2.4 and 5 GHz) networks

- **Audio:** Three 2" (51 mm) midrange speakers, one 1" (25 mm) tweeter, one 5.25" (133 mm) woofer with bass aperture to maximise bass output.

- **Output:** 3.5 mm stereo audio, & mini-optical line in

- **Colours:** Charcoal

Echo Auto

Interact with Alexa in your car...

Using the Echo Auto, you can communicate with Alexa while driving, so you can use your voice to play music, check the news, make calls, add to your to-do-list, set reminders, pay for gas, and more. The Echo Auto connects to the Alexa app on your phone, then plays through your car's speakers via auxiliary input or your smartphone's Bluetooth connection. A Vent Mount is also included, so you can easily attach the Echo Auto to an air vent within your vehicle.

Specifications:

- **Size:** 104 mm x 97 mm x 91 mm (4.1" x 3.8" x 3.6")
- **Weight:** 420 grams
- **Wi-Fi:** Wi-Fi: Dual-band 802.11 a/b/g/n/ac (2.4 and 5 GHz) networks
- **Audio:** 1.6" speaker
- **Output:** 3.5 mm stereo audio
- **Colours:** Charcoal, Glacier White, PRODUCT(RED), Twilight Blue

Echo Buds

Take Alexa with you, even during a workout...

With the Echo Buds, you can communicate with Alexa, stream music, play podcasts, and read Audible audiobooks, all via a Bluetooth connection with the Alexa app on your smartphone. Echo Buds are small, light, and sweat-resistant, with a secure, customizable fit that's made to move with you.

Specifications:

- **Size:** 144 x 144 x 133 mm (5.0" x 5.0" x 4.7")
- **Weight:** 970 grams
- **Wi-Fi:** Dual-band 802.11 a/b/g/n/ac (2.4 and 5 GHz) networks
- **Audio:** 3" neodymium woofer and 2 x 0.8" tweeters
- **Output:** 3.5 mm stereo audio
- **Colours:** Charcoal, Glacier White, PRODUCT(RED), Twilight Blue

Still wondering which Echo to get?

Here are some tips to help you choose...

The Echo is the most popular smart speaker in the world, but it comes in a variety of sizes, colours, and specifications. Choosing the right one for you isn't just determined by cost, but also where you plan to locate your Echo and what you hope to use it for. Here are some tips and pointers to help you decide...

"All I need is the basics"

If you want an inexpensive Echo device to ask Alexa questions and listen to music, then the Echo Dot is the device for you. It's small, affordable, and still packs a powerful speaker for listening to music.

"I want to place my Echo in the kitchen"

Look for an Echo device that includes a screen. The Echo Show might be the perfect choice, as it's small enough to tuck in a corner, and it has a display for offering recipe and cooking suggestions.

"I spend a lot of time communicating with friends and family"

The Echo Show would be a great option, as the touchscreen is large enough to see friends and family clearly, but for the ultimate experience, go for the Echo Show 10. It features a large 10.1-inch display that can swivel automatically to follow you around the room, so you never wander out of the camera view.

"I'm all about music. The louder the better!"

There's only one choice if you love your music: the Echo Studio. It has five powerful speakers that can fill any room, and can sense the acoustics of your space to fine-tune playback for optimal sound.

"I like to control the smart devices scattered throughout my home"

If you live in a large home with smart device such as lights, thermostats, and camera, then it's a great idea to have Echo devices in each room. This way, you can always control your smart devices without having to shout. To keep things affordable, opt for multiple Echo Dots, and you'll be good to go.

Chapter 02

Setting up

So you've purchased an Echo device from Amazon. What next? Surprisingly, there's quite a lot to do. Before Alexa can work it needs to connect to the internet, and to do that, you'll need a smartphone or tablet to hand. Don't worry, as all of this is explained over the next few pages. As are the basics controls of an Echo, how to set up and customise your Echo, and how to connect external speakers.

In this chapter:

The Echo hardware

What the buttons do, and what the colours mean...

Before we get started with your Journey with Alexa, it's a good idea to take a look at the hardware used to bring it to life. It's very likely that you've purchased an Echo device from Amazon (see the last chapter for an overview on each). Once you've unboxed your Echo, you'll notice that it has a few buttons on the top and a light ring circling its circumference. Over the following two pages, we'll explore what these buttons do and what the ling ring indicates using colour and movement.

Echo buttons

Most Echo devices have the following buttons located on their top:

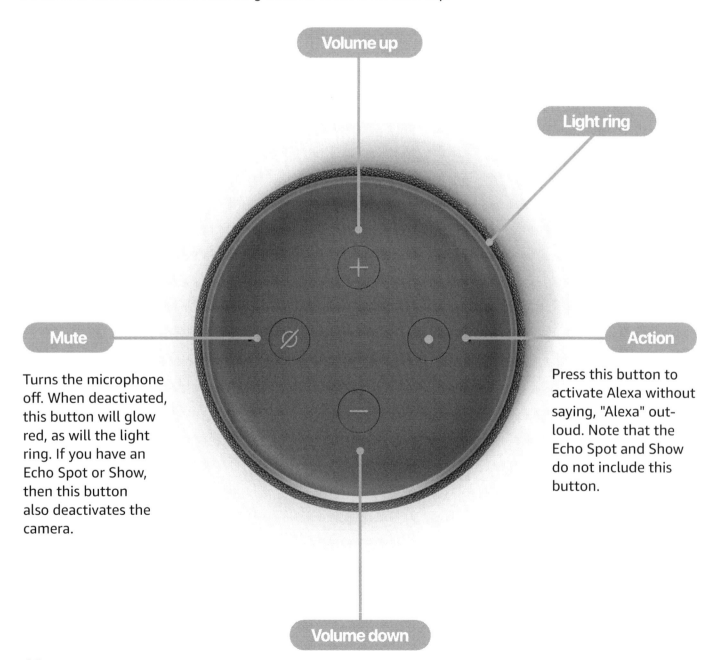

Volume up

Light ring

Mute

Turns the microphone off. When deactivated, this button will glow red, as will the light ring. If you have an Echo Spot or Show, then this button also deactivates the camera.

Action

Press this button to activate Alexa without saying, "Alexa" out-loud. Note that the Echo Spot and Show do not include this button.

Volume down

The light ring

Circling the 4th generation Echo, Echo Dot, and Echo Studio is a light ring that runs the entire circumference of the device. It comes to life in several ways and colours, depending on the context of the situation. The Echo Show, with its large touchscreen, also features a version of the light ring, but it's a strip of coloured light that runs along the bottom of the screen when active. Here's what each light ring animation and colour means:

○ **No light:** Alexa is inactive and waiting for your next command.

○ **Blue, with a spinning cyan arc:** The Echo device is starting up.

○ **Blue, with a stationary cyan arc:** Alexa is listening and processing your command. The cyan part of the ring will be pointed towards the person talking.

○ **Alternating blue and cyan:** Alexa has submitted your command and is waiting for a response.

○ **Red:** The microphone is turned off.

○ **Pulsing yellow:** A message or notification is waiting for you.

○ **Pulsing green:** There's an incoming call or Drop In.

○ **Spinning green:** Your in a call or Drop In.

○ **Pulsing white:** The volume is being adjusted, with the more white you see, the louder the volume.

○ **Spinning orange:** The Echo is in setup mode.

○ **Pulsing purple:** There is no Wi-Fi connection.

○ **A flash of purple:** No Not Disturb mode is activated.

Install the Alexa app

To make the most out of Alexa, you'll need the app...

In an ideal world, you could simply take your Echo out of the box, push the power button, and start asking Alexa questions. Unfortunately, things are not so simple. That's because Alexa needs to connect to the internet. It needs to do this so that anything you say can be processed and understood before a response is sent back and played through the Echo's speakers. It also needs to know your name and address (for things like ordering items on Amazon or giving you a weather report), and it needs to know which account to use for playing music.

All of this is set up via the Amazon Alexa app, which is free for most smartphones and tablets. Think of the Alexa app as the key to starting your journey with Alexa, because without the app, Alexa can't get started. Here's how to find the app, set it up, and understand the basics...

Amazon Alexa app requirements

Here's what you need to install the Alexa app:

- An iPhone or iPad running iOS 11 or later

- An Android phone or tablet running Android 5 or later

- An Amazon Fire tablet running Fire OS 3 or later

How to install and set up the Alexa app

If your device meets the requirements above, open the App Store and search for "Alexa". The first result will be the Alexa app you need. Download and open it, then sign in to your Amazon account by following these steps:

1 In the **Email** field, enter the email address used for your Amazon account. If you use a mobile phone number to log into Amazon, then you can also use this number. If you don't have an Amazon account yet, then tap the **Create a New Amazon Account** button, then follow the on-screen instructions.

2 In the **Amazon password** field, type your Amazon account password.

3 Tap **Sign-In**. If you have two-factor authentification enabled, then you may be asked to enter a six-digit code, which will be texted to your mobile phone.

4 Tap **I'm [name]**, where **[name]** is the username associated with your Amazon account. If you'd like to use a different name, or if you're someone else, then tap **I'm somone else**, enter a name, then tap **Continue**.

5 You will then be logged into the Amazon Alexa app, where you'll be presented with the screen across the page...

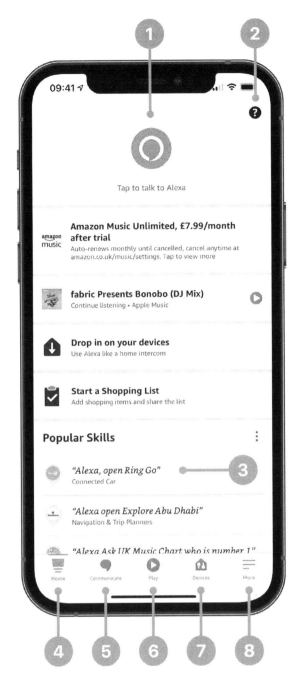

Exploring the Amazon Alexa app

Here's a quick overview of the Amazon Alexa app on a smartphone:

1 Tap on the **blue circle**, or say, "Alexa" out-loud, to perform a command.

2 Tap this button to contact Amazon, provide feedback, or explore help topics.

3 Explore Skills available for Alexa by browsing this area. Scroll down to discover topics and additional features.

4 Tap **Home** to return to this screen at any time.

5 Tap **Communicate** to make a phone call, send a text message, or drop in on another Alexa device.

6 Tap **Play** to listen to music on Amazon Music, radio stations, Kindle books, or podcasts.

7 Tap **Devices** to set up or configure an Echo, or control smart devices within your home.

8 Tap **More** to access your lists and notes, alarms and timers, routines, or alter settings.

Dig a little deeper...

See your Alexa contacts

After sharing your contacts with Alexa (see Communication chapter), you can quickly get in touch with someone by tapping **Communicate**, then the **group** icon in the top-right corner.

Customise an Echo device

By using the Alexa app, you can adjust a number of settings on each of your Echo devices. To see these settings, tap **Devices** at the bottom of the screen, tap **Echo & Alexa**, then choose a device.

Access additional settings

While using the Alexa app, tap **More** in the bottom corner, then **Settings**. On the following panel, you'll be able to adjust a massive number of settings, including account settings, device settings, and privacy.

Set up your Echo

With the app installed, it's time to set up your device...

O n the previous two pages, we looked at the Amazon Alexa app and how it works like a key to starting your journey with Alexa. Now that you've downloaded, installed, and set up the app, it's time to set up your Amazon Echo, the physical object that you'll spend the next weeks, months, and maybe even years talking to.

Where to place your Echo

For your Echo device to work at its best, you should carefully think about the best place to keep it in the house. There are a few things to consider:

- If there are multiple people in your house, try to place the Echo where everyone usually gathers.

- Make sure there's a plug socket nearby to power your Echo.

- Alexa requires a Wi-Fi signal to work, so don't place the Echo too far away from your router.

Once you've figured out the best place, it's time to unbox your Echo and turn it on for the first time. Simply plug the power cord into the Echo, and it will automatically turn on for the first time.

How to set up an Echo with a screen

If your Echo comes with a touchscreen, then you can get it up and running by using its display. Here's how it works:

1 After your Echo has booted up, it will ask for your Wi-Fi details. Use the touchscreen to select your Wi-Fi network, then enter its password using the on-screen keyboard. If you don't know this, then try looking on the back of the Wi-Fi router. Usually a sticker can be found which contains the Wi-Fi password. You can also try asking whoever set up the Wi-Fi connection.

2 Tap **Next**, and if you've entered your password correctly, your Echo will connect to the web and automatically add itself as a device within the Alexa app on your smartphone. You're now good to go..

How to set up an Echo without a screen

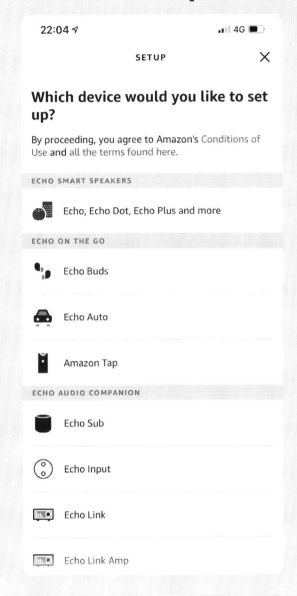

If your Echo doesn't have a touchscreen, then you'll need to use the Amazon Alexa app to set up your device. To do this, open the app and then:

1. Tap **Devices** at the bottom of the screen, then tap the **plus** button in the top-right corner.

2. A panel will slide up from the bottom of the screen. Tap **Add Device**.

3. Tap the type of device you're adding. It's very likely to be an **Amazon Echo**.

4. On the following screen, tap the option near the top that says **Echo, Echo Dot, Echo Plus and more**.

5. On the following screen, confirm that your Echo is plugged in and in set up mode. If it is, then you should see an orange ring spinning around the device.

6. The app will then look for nearby Echo devices in setup mode. Once yours appears, tap on it.

7. If the app asks for your Wi-Fi details, tap on your network, enter its password, then tap **Connect**.

8. The app will then connect your Echo to your Wi-Fi network. Tap **Continue** when prompted, then follow any further instructions to set up your Echo.

Customise your Echo

Set the time, location, language, and much more...

Before we get to the fun stuff (actually talking to your Alexa), it's worth taking a few moments to ensure everything is set up correctly. For example, it's possible to change the default langauge, location, measurements of units, and even create a custom voice profile so that Alexa recognises you in a multiple household.

Change the default language or accent

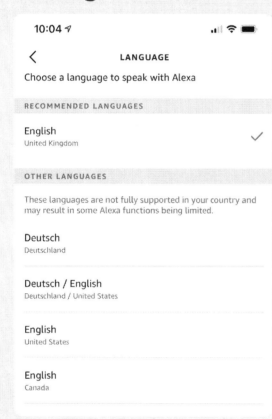

Alexa will talk to you in the language used for your Amazon account, so if you're registered with Amazon.com, you'll hear an American accent, and if you're registered with Amazon.fr, you'll talk to Alexa in French. To change the language Alexa uses to communicate, open the Alexa app on your smartphone or tablet and then:

1. Tap **Devices** at the bottom of the screen, then select your Echo device.

2. Scroll down and tap **Language**.

3. The Alexa app will then display every language available for your device.

4. Select another language (or accent). The app will warn that the selected language might not be fully supported in your country. Tap **OK** if you wish to continue.

5. Your Echo will then update, and you'll hear the new language or accent next time you interact with Alexa.

Ask Alexa to learn your voice

If there are multiple people in your house, then you can ask Alexa to learn each voice, enabling it to recognise individuals within a household. This is helpful for when you're making purchases on Amazon, making a voice call, or sending a text message.

When you're ready to ask Alexa to learn your voice, first make sure that there are no background noises and that only once Echo device is within earshot. Next, say, "*Alexa, learn my voice*". Alexa will then greet you and you to repeat a few sentences, such as, "*Alexa, search for holiday music*". Once your voice has been recognised, you can get other household members to repeat the process.

Change the device location

Alexa will use the address saved in your Amazon account to give you accurate weather forecasts and traffic conditions, but if you'd rather use a different location, then here's how to change it:

1 Open the Alexa app on your smartphone or tablet, tap **Devices** at the bottom of the screen, then select your Echo device.

2 Tap **Device Location**.

3 To change the country, tap CHANGE near the top of the screen, then use the scroll wheel to select a new country.

4 To edit the actual address, use the form fields to alter the physical address and post/zip code.

5 Tap **Save** when you're finished, and the device will be updated to reflect your changes.

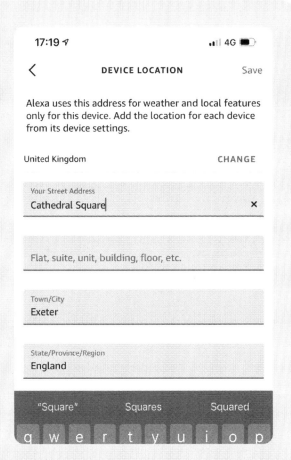

Change the time zone

Your Echo will default to the time zone in your physical address, but if you're working with a time overseas or doing a set of night shifts, it can be helpful to change the time zone to somewhere else in the world. To do this:

1 Open the Alexa app on your smartphone or tablet, tap **Devices** at the bottom of the screen, then select your Echo device.

2 Scroll down, then tap **Time Zone**.

3 To specify a different part of the world, tap **CHANGE** near the top of the screen, then use the scroll wheel to select another continent.

4 To select a country within your overall time zone, select a country and daylight time zone using the list.

5 The Alexa app will warn you that any change might affect any existing alarms you have. Tap **OK** to confirm. Your Echo will then adjust to the new time zone of your choice.

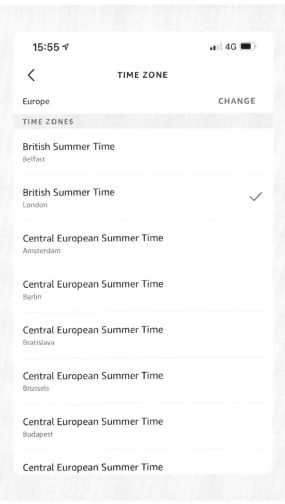

Change measurement units

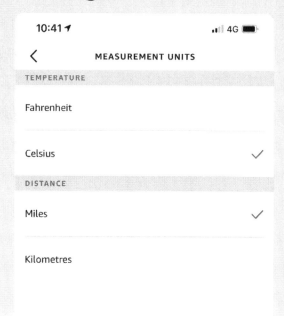

Your Echo device will default its measurement of units based on your physical location. This means if you're in the United States, you'll get weather reports in Fahrenheit and distance in kilometres, while in the UK, you'll get celsius and miles. If you'd like to override these defaults:

1 Open the Alexa app on your smartphone or tablet, tap **Devices** at the bottom of the screen, then select your Echo device.

2 Scroll down and tap **Measurement Units**.

3 Update the settings to reflect your needs, then tap the **back arrow** to save.

4 Your Echo will then update, and you'll hear revised measurement units next time you interact with Alexa.

Customise the Home Screen of your Echo Show

If you have an Echo Show, then it's possible to display a wide range of information panels on the display, including calendar events, communication alerts, recent scores for your favourite teams, plus much more. To toggle these on or off:

1 Swipe down from the top of your Echo Show display, then tap **Settings**.

2 Scroll down, then tap **Home Content**.

3 Toggle "on" any content you'd like to see on the display. The next time any updates arrive from your chosen settings, then they will appear on the Home Screen of your Echo.

Customise the wallpaper and clock on Echo Show

By default, the Echo Show will cycle through various wallpaper subjects such as art and nature, while occasionally displaying news and weather updates. To customise this:

1. Swipe down from the top of your Echo Show display, then tap **Settings**.

2. Scroll down, then tap **Wallpaper & Clock**.

3. To use your own photos (see below for more details) toggle "on" one of the top three options. To choose a wallpaper theme, scroll down and make an option. To customise the clock settings, scroll down futher and make a choice.

Turn your Echo Show into a slideshow

The Echo Show is the perfect way to display your photos as an animated slideshow, thanks to its bright and colourful screen. You'll need to use the Amazon Alexa app to set this up, but it only takes a few moments. Here's how it works:

1. Open the Alexa app on your smartphone or tablet, tap **Devices** at the bottom of the screen, then select your Echo Show.

2. Scroll down, then tap **Home Content**.

3. To use images saved on your smartphone, tap **Manually select my photos**, then **Continue**.

4. The app will ask for permission to access your photos. Tap **Yes**, or Allow Access.

5. Select the photos you wish to display on your Echo Show. You can select a maximum of 10 in one go. Tap **Add** when you've finished.

6. The photos will then be uploaded to your Amazon Photos account. As they finish uploading, you'll see them appear on the Home Screen of your Echo Show.

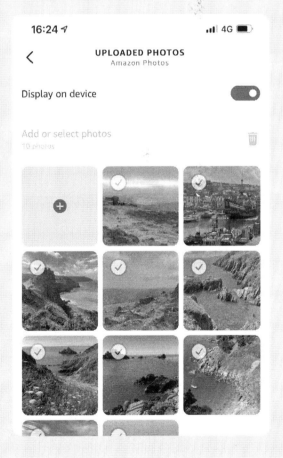

Connect a set of external speakers

Both the Echo Studio and Echo Show have amazing speakers that will fill almost any room with a clear, punchy sound. If you have an Echo Dot, however, then you might not find the audio quality good enough, or loud enough, to blow anyone away. That's where a pair of wired, external speakers come into play. By connecting a set of speakers to your Echo, you can ensure any audio playback is loud, clear, and bassy.

All Echo devices come with a 3.5 mm audio output port around the back. It's the smaller of the two round ports. Here's where to find it on the Echo Dot and Show:

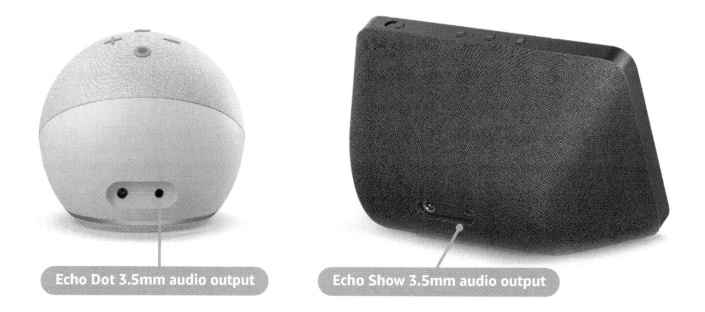

Echo Dot 3.5mm audio output

Echo Show 3.5mm audio output

To connect the speakers, plug the 3.5mm cable (the same cable you'll find included with headphones and other audio-based devices) into the audio output port, then plug the speakers into a power socket. To avoid any audio interference, try to place the speakers at least three feet from your Echo. Once plugged in and powered up, your Echo will automatically play audio through the speakers.

Connect a pair of Bluetooth speakers

While wired speakers are great for listening to Alexa (and media content) from a fixed point, Bluetooth speakers offer much more flexibility. Not only are they wireless, but you can also get Bluetooth headphones with built-in microphones, which means you can interact with Alexa while moving around the home.

There are some minor restrictions with using a Bluetooth speaker with an Echo device, primarily in that an Echo device can only connect to one Bluetooth device at a time. It's also slightly fiddly to set up as we explore across the page...

Step 1: put your Bluetooth speaker into pairing mode

For your Echo to find a Bluetooth device, that device needs to be in pairing mode. When in this mode, the device sounds out a wireless "ping" to let other devices know that they can connect.

Every Bluetooth device has its own way of going into pairing mode. Usually, there's a specific button that you can press and hold for a few seconds - take a look at your speaker's instruction manual if you're unsure.

Step 2: use the Alexa app to connect your Echo

With your Bluetooth speaker in pairing mode, grab your smartphone or tablet and open the Amazon Alexa app, then:

1. Tap **Devices** at the bottom of the screen, then select the Echo device that you would like to pair.

2. Look for the CONNECTED DEVICES area, then where it says Speaker, tap **Change**.

3. Tap **Bluetooth**, choose **NEXT**, then tap **PAIR A NEW DEVICE**.

4. The Echo will start looking for nearby Bluetooth devices in pairing mode. This may only take a few seconds or up to a minute. When your speaker or headphones appear, tap on it, and the Echo will say, "connected".

Reconnect to a Bluetooth device

Some Bluetooth devices will automatically connect to your Echo whenever they are powered up, while others (such as a smartphone) will only connect when playing audio. If you've already paired a Bluetooth device, but it's not connected, stand near your Echo and say:

"Alexa, connect"

After a moment or two, your Echo will reconnect to the Bluetooth device.

Disconnect a Bluetooth device

If you no longer want to play audio through a Bluetooth speaker, open the Amazon Alexa app and then:

1. Tap **Devices** at the bottom of the screen, then select the Echo device you would like to unpair.

2. Tap **Bluetooth Devices**.

3. Look for the paired device, tap the small **down arrow** to its right, then tap **Forget Device**.

4. After a moment or two, your Echo will disconnect from the Bluetooth speaker.

Chapter 03

Get to Know Alexa

So you've learned how Alexa works, the many devices supported by it, and how to set up an Echo. Now it's time to start getting to Alexa. In this chapter, you'll learn the basic commands used to control Alexa, then explore how to ask general questions, get information about the world around you, and even translate languages.

In this chapter:

Get to know Alexa

Now that you've set up your Echo, it's time to start talking to Alexa...

With your Echo device set up and powered on, you're finally ready to take your first steps into Alexa's world. Or rather, Alexa is now ready to listen to your voice and start performing commands. Keep in mind that Alexa isn't listening to everything you say, instead, it responds to a single keyword that you need to say out loud:

"Alexa..."

With that one word, Alexa springs into life, emits a chime, and displays a blue glow around the light ring. If you're trying to stay quiet (for example, if everyone else in the house is asleep), then you can also whisper, "*Alexa*", or press the **Action** button on the top of your Echo.

Now that you've got Alexa's attention, it's time to issue a command. We'll cover a wide range of these over the next few pages, but to give an example, you could say:

"Alexa, give me the news"

After a moment or two, Alexa will give you a daily Flash Briefing, which includes the latest news and weather for your area.

Tell Alexa to be quiet

If Alexa is going *on and on* about a particular subject or question, then you can ask her to stop talking by saying one of these commands...

"Alexa, stop"   "Alexa, mute"

"Alexa, enough"   "Alexa, cancel"

"Alexa, thank you"   "Alexa, sleep"

A few commands to get you going

You can ask Alexa literally anything, and chances are she'll have the answer. Over the next few pages, we explore the commands you can use to ask for information, answers mathematic questions, and even convert units. Later in the book, we also dive deep into sending messages, controlling media, and much more; but for now, here are a few basic commands that you can try:

"Alexa, what's the weather like?"

"Alexa, what's the time?"

"Alexa, what date is it?"

"Alexa, how's the traffic?"

"Alexa, where's the nearest store?"

"Alexa, what movies are playing?"

"Alexa, play [song or album]"

"Alexa, play [audiobook]"

"Alexa, set an alarm for [time]"

"Alexa, wake me up every weekday at [time]"

"Alexa, what's on my calendar?"

"Alexa, what time does the sun set?"

"Alexa, call [name]"

"Alexa, message [name]"

"Alexa, order [item]"

"Alexa, where's my stuff?"

"Alexa, turn [device] on"

Use Follow-Up Mode to keep the conversation

Whenever you interact with Alexa, you need to say, "Alexa..." out loud before each command. If you like to issue multiple commands (for example, turning on individual lights within the house), then you can activate Follow-Up Mode. When this is enabled, you only have to say "Alexa" once and then issue multiple commands. To turn on Follow-Up Mode:

1. Open the Alexa app on your smartphone or tablet, tap **Devices** at the bottom of the screen, then select your Echo.

2. Scroll down, then tap **Follow-Up Mode**.

3. On the following screen, toggle **Follow-Up Mode** on, and your Echo device will now be ready for you to issue multiple commands.

Ask general questions

Alexa knows a lot about the world...

Long before the internet was available in nearly every home, finding the answer to a simple question involved asking someone else face-to-face, searching through encyclopedias, or as a last resort, taking a guess. Thankfully, Alexa knows the answer to pretty much anything you can think of. Want to know how many teeth a cat has? Alexa knows! Want to know if a disease is contagious? You guessed it, Alexa knows!

Over the next few pages, we'll take a look at all the various categories of questions you can ask Alexa, from the scientific to the downright silly. Keep in mind that Alexa knows pretty much everything, so if you don't see the question in this book, try asking anyway...

Ask general knowledge questions

If there's something on your mind, try saying...

"Alexa, how tall is Mount Everest?"

"Alexa, how hot is the sun?"

"Alexa, how tall is an Oak tree?"

"Alexa, what's the fastest animal?"

"Alexa, how many teeth does a shark have?"

"Alexa, when did the Titanic sink?"

"Alexa, what's the most successful computer game of all time?"

"Alexa, what side of the road should I drive on?"

"Alexa, why is an orange orange?"

"Alexa, who built the pyramids?"

"Alexa, where does rain come from?"

"Alexa, how tall is the average person?"

"Alexa, what's the name of the longest river in South America?"

"Alexa, why do people get goosebumps?"

"Alexa, which paintings did Van Gogh paint?"

"Alexa, how far is America from Europe?"

"Alexa, what is a jackfruit?"

"Alexa, what's the temperature of boiling water?"

Find out what's nearby

If you're new to the area, ask Alexa for nearby places...

Because Alexa knows your home address, it can find nearby restaurants, coffee shops, and even dentists. It can also tell you the opening hours of these locations, how far away they are, and what their contact information is. When you're ready to learn about nearby places, try saying..

"Alexa, what [businesses] are nearby?"

"Alexa, where's the nearest [business]?" For example, "Alexa, where's the nearest Starbucks?"

"Alexa, what's the address for [business]?"

"Alexa, what's the phone number for [business]?"

"Alexa, is [business] open?"

"Alexa, what are the opening hours for [business]?

"Alexa, how far away is [business]?"

"Alexa, where can I get [product]?" For example, "Alexa, where can I get sushi?"

Convert units

Turn kilograms into pounds, or degrees into C...

For reasons that often seem inexplicable, measurements, weights, currencies, and temperatures are all measured differently depending on where you live (or how old you are). For those times when you need to turn teaspoons into ounces, try saying:

"Alexa, how many [units] are in [number] of [units]?"

"Alexa, what's [number] [units] in [units]?

For example:

"Alexa, how many litres are in 15 gallons?"

"Alexa, what's 75 degrees Fahrenheit in celsius?"

"Alexa, how much is 15 pounds in US dollars?"

"Alexa, how many kilometres are in 2 miles?"

Perform calculations

Ask Alexa to sum it up...

If you don't have a calculator to hand and can't work out the calculation yourself, then Alexa is pretty good at maths. Here are some of the things you can ask:

"Alexa, what's [number] [operator] [number]?"

For example:

"Alexa, what's 15 times 20?"

"Alexa, what's 98 divided by 7?"

"Alexa, what's 20 squared?"

"Alexa, what's 40 cubed?"

"Alexa, what's 20 to the power of 10?"

"Alexa, what's the square root of 50?"

"Alexa, what's the cube root of 75?"

"Alexa, what's 12 factorial?"

"Alexa, what's the tangent of 100?"

"Alexa, pick a random number between [number 1] and [number 2]"

"Alexa, what's the value of PI?"

"Alexa, what's the value of e?"

Ask Alexa about science

Expand your knowledge...

If you'd like a quick overview of a scientific topic, try asking Alexa. You can also ask specific questions, and Alexa will let you know the answer straight away. Here are just a few:

"Alexa, what is [topic]?"

"Alexa, how old is the Earth?"

"Alexa, what's the nearest star?"

"Alexa, what is aluminium?"

"Alexa, who invented the internet?"

"Alexa, what's the biggest mammal?"

"Alexa, who won the Nobel Peace Prize in 2020?"

"Alexa, what's the chemical symbol for gold?"

"Alexa, which animal lives the longest?"

"Alexa, how does Wi-Fi work?"

Dates and times

Wondering when something is going to happen?...

It's easy to lose track of time. Sometimes the days fly by, while at other days they can't come quickly enough. However you're keeping time, here are some questions you can ask Alexa about dates and time:

"Alexa, how many days until [date]?"

"Alexa, how long is it until Christmas?"

"Alexa, how many days until [holiday]?"

"Alexa, how many days has it been since [date]?"

"Alexa, when is the first day of [season]?"

"Alexa, when is the [solice or equinox]?"

"Alexa, when is the next full moon?"

"Alexa, when is the next high tide?"

"Alexa, what time is sunset?"

"Alexa, how long has it been since [date]?"

"Alexa, what day is on [date]?"

Ask Alexa about culture

Broaden your horizons...

Whether you want to learn more about a celebrity, the latest social media craze, or a priceless painting, Alexa has all the answers. Here are a few suggestions you can try:

"Alexa, which movies has [actor] been in?"

"Alexa, who won this year's Oscar for best actress?"

"Alexa, who painted The Last Supper?"

"Alexa, when did WW1 start?"

"Alexa, what language is spoken in Chile?"

"Alexa, when was Albert Einstein born?"

"Alexa, who is the Priminister of the United Kingdom?"

"Alexa, how old is [name]?"

Linguistic questions

Struggling to think of a word? Alexa can help...

Sometimes it can be difficult to think of a suitable replacement for a word. Usually, you'd grab a thesaurus and start browsing, but it's much easier to just ask Alexa:

"Alexa, give me another word for [word]"

"Alexa, what's the opposite of [word]?"

"Alexa, how do you spell [word]?"

"Alexa, what's the definition of [word]?"

"Alexa, what rhymes with [word]?"

"Alexa, how many letters are in the word [word]?

Translate language

Communicate in another language...

Not only does Alexa know how to find alternative words, but it can also translate words and even entire sentences, making it possible to talk to someone from another country or culture. At the time of writing (May 2021), Alexa can translate between English and Spanish, German, French, Hindi, Italian, and Brazilian Portuguese. To begin, say:

"Alexa, translate [language]"

Then tell Alexa what to translate. When you're finished, say, "Alexa, stop". Alternative translation commands include:

"Alexa, how do you say [word] in [language]?"

"Alexa, translate [word] in [language]"

"Alexa, what's the word for [word] in [language]?"

Get sports updates

Stay up to date with your favourite team...

Alexa is quite a sports fan, and keeps up to date on nearly every football match, Tennis game, and championship. To make sure you never miss a score or match result, try asking Alexa:

"Alexa, what's the score of the [team name] game?"

"Alexa, who won the [team or event] game?"

"Alexa, who is winning the [event] game?"

"Alexa, what was the score of the [team or event] game?"

"Alexa, when do the [team] play next?"

"Alexa, when is the next [team] game?"

"Alexa, did [team] win?"

"Alexa, how are the [team] doing?"

Chapter 04

Music, audiobooks, and video

Y ou might not think of Alexa as an all-encompassing media device, but if you have an Echo with a touchscreen, then that's precisely what Alexa can be. Using an Echo Show, you can watch Amazon Prime content, YouTube videos, and Netflix. Every Echo device can also listen to audiobooks, podcasts, and music from your favourite content providers such as Amazon Music and Apple Music.

There's quite a lot to cover in this chapter, including music-based commands, the Amazon Music app, plus how to stream content from your smartphone or tablet.

In this chapter:

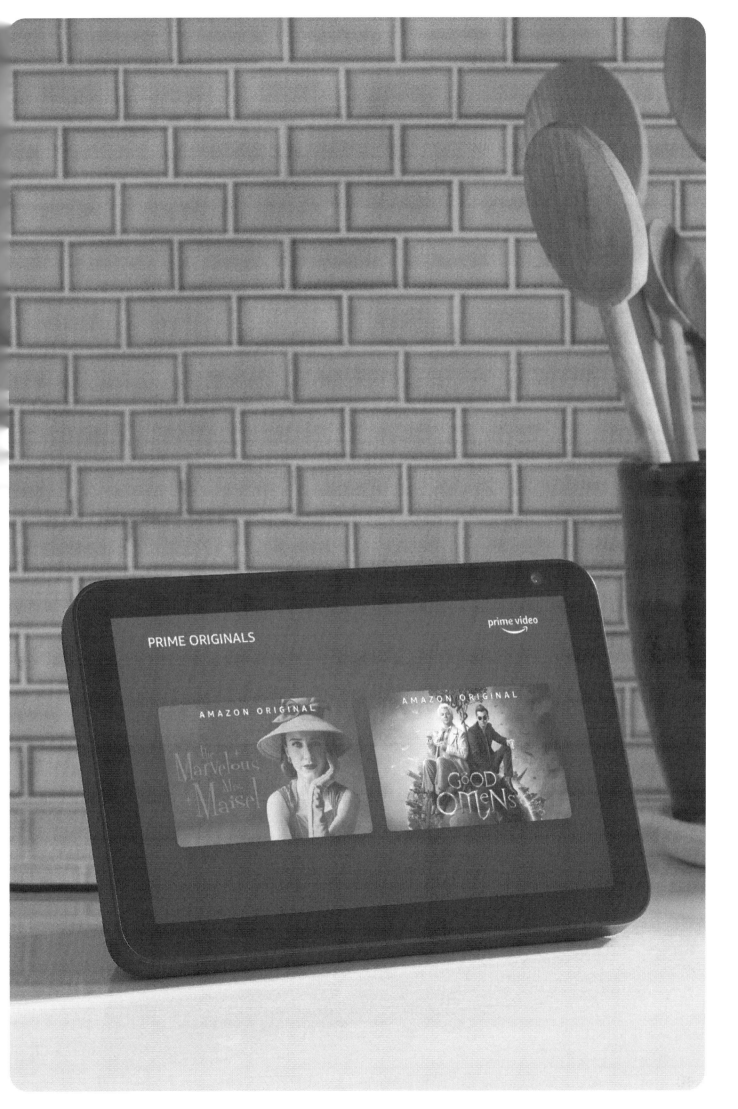

Music: set up your Alexa

Learn how to set up music playback on your Alexa...

One of the most popular skills Alexa can do is play music. It makes sense when you think about it, as Alexa is an audio-based service, with each device serving as a large speaker for your home. Thanks to its clever voice recognition and uncanny ability to recognise commands, you can easily play a song, album, or playlist without getting off the couch.

Before you start issuing commands, you need to decide how you want to play music through your Alexa. There are two choices to make:

Use an Alexa-supported music service

Once you've set up your Alexa (see "Link to a music service" below), it will automatically play music from Amazon Music, but you can also use Spotify, Apple Music, TuneIn, or Deezer. This list might change depending on your location.

Use your mobile or a tablet to play music

You can stream music wirelessly from your phone or tablet straight to Alexa. This is a helpful option if your music provider of choice isn't supported by Alexa.

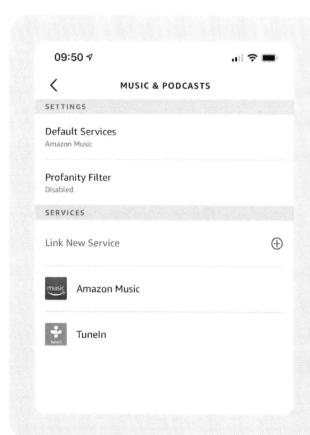

Link to a music service

You can ask Alexa to play music from a small number of music providers that are based on your location. Some require you to have a subscription before they can work with Alexa. Spotify, for example, only works with Alexa if you have a Spotify Premium subscription.

To link one of these music services to your Alexa:

1. Open the Alexa app on your phone or tablet. Tap **More**, then choose **Settings**.

2. Tap **Music & Podcasts**. You might see Amazon Music already set up. You can leave this and play music straight away, or you can tap **Link New Service** to choose another service.

3. Tap the service of choice, then follow the instructions to log into the music service and authorise Alexa.

Change the default music service

Your Alexa will automatically connect to Amazon Music once it is set up. If you'd like to use a different service (such as Apple Music), then here are the steps you need to take to change the default music service:

1 Open the Alexa app on your phone or tablet. Tap **More**, then choose **Settings**.

2 Tap **Music & Podcasts**, then **Default Services**.

3 To change the default service for music playback, tap **Change** under the Music section, then make a choice.

4 Similarly, to change the default service for Artists, Genres, and Podcasts, tap the **Change** button for each section.

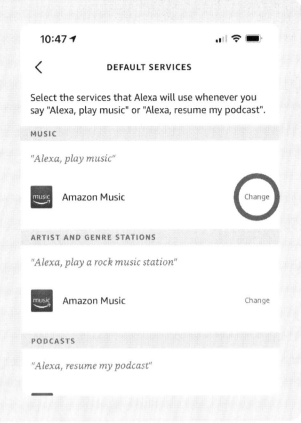

Stream music from your phone or tablet

Rather than stream audio from a music service, you can use a Bluetooth to play music on your smartphone or tablet and hear it through your Alexa's speaker. To do this:

1 Open the Alexa app on your phone or tablet. Tap **Devices** > **Echo & Alexa**, then tap the Alexa device you wish to use.

2 Under the **Connected Devices** section, tap **Change** > **Bluetooth**, then **Next**.

3 Tap **Pair a New Device**. Your Alexa is now in pairing mode.

4 Close the Alexa app, then using your phone or tablet, open the Bluetooth settings. If you're using an iPhone, open the **Settings** app then choose **Bluetooth**. On an Android device, open **Settings**, choose **Connections**, then **Bluetooth**.

5 After a short wait you should see your Alexa appear. Tap on it to pair the two devices.

With pairing complete, any audio you play on your phone or tablet will play through Alexa's speakers. You can also reconnect to your phone in the future by saying "Alexa, connect to my phone".

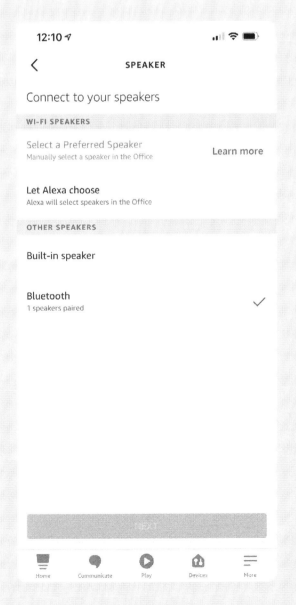

Music commands

Tell Alexa to play, pause, and skip...

Now that you've told Alexa which sources of music to play from, it's time to start listening to your favourite artists, bands, and playlists. Alexa has a massive amount of voice commands for controlling music playback, but don't worry, as they're all intuitive and easy to remember. Before we get started, however, there are a few things to keep in mind:

Not all commands work with every service

Most will, but you might find that one command works on Apple Music, but not on Spotify.

You can replace the word *song* with a *track* or *tune*

Don't worry if that sounds like a riddle. It basically means that if you see the word *song* in the commands covered over the next few pages, you can often replace it with a track name or tune.

Alexa will remember what you listened to

This means that if you listened to a song recently but can't remember its name, you can say something like "Alexa, play that Coldplay song I was listening to yesterday," or, "Alexa, play Rihanna songs I haven't heard in a while."

Play music

To get you started, here are some commands for playing music...

"Alexa, play music by [artist]"

"Alexa, play [artists] latest album"

"Alexa, play the song [title]"

"Alexa, play the album [title]"

"Alexa, play [song, album, or playlist title]"

"Alexa, play the song I just bought"

"Alexa, play the song that goes [lyrics]. For example, "Alexa, play the song that goes ' Ground Control to Major Tom'"

Adjust the volume

If the music's too loud (or quiet), then here's how to adjust it...

"Alexa, turn up (or down)"

"Alexa, volume up (or down)"

"Alexa, louder (or quieter)"

"Alexa, softer"

"Alexa, set the volume to [number from 1 to 10]"

"Alexa, mute"

"Alexa, unmute"

Control music playback

While Alexa is playing music, you can use the following commands to control playback...

"Alexa, stop"

"Alexa, pause"

"Alexa, play"

"Alexa, resume"

"Alexa, next"

"Alexa, previous"

"Alexa, turn repeat on"

"Alexa, turn repeat off"

"Alexa, turn shuffle on (or off)"

"Alexa, skip back [number] seconds"

"Alexa, skip forward [number] seconds"

"Alexa, restart song"

"Alexa, play again"

"Alexa, restart album"

"Alexa, restart playlist"

Find new music

When you're ready to try something new, here are some commands for finding new music...

"Alexa, play new music by [artist]"

"Alexa, play some new music"

"Alexa, play something new"

"Alexa, play new [genre] music"

"Alexa, play [artist] station"

"Alexa, play songs similar to [title]"

"Alexa, play music similar to this"

"Alexa, play [artist] songs I've never heard"

Play music by era or genre

You can ask Alexa to play music based on a number of genres...

"Alexa, play music from the '50s"   "Alexa, play Christian music"

"Alexa, play music from the '90s"   "Alexa, play movie soundtracks"

"Alexa, play country music"   "Alexa, play vocal music"

"Alexa, play pop music"   "Alexa, play jazz music"

"Alexa, play classical music"   "Alexa, play children's music"

"Alexa, play classic rock music"   "Alexa, play easy listening music"

Play music by mood or activity

If you're feeling in a particular mood, then here are some commands you can try...

"Alexa, play happy music"   "Alexa, play dinner music"

"Alexa, play laid back music"   "Alexa, play sleep music"

"Alexa, play mellow music"   "Alexa, play partying music"

"Alexa, play chill music"   "Alexa, play working music"

"Alexa, play romantic music"   "Alexa, play jogging music"

"Alexa, play upbeat music"   "Alexa, play relaxing music"

"Alexa, play angry music"   "Alexa, play cooking music"

"Alexa, play sad music"   "Alexa, play reading music"

"Alexa, play energetic music"   "Alexa, play working out music"

"Alexa, play feeling good music"   "Alexa, play studying music"

Find popular music

See what everyone else is listening too, even in other countries...

"Alexa, play the top songs"

"Alexa, play the top 10"

"Alexa, play the top songs from the [decade]"

"Alexa, play the top songs from [country]"

"Alexa, play the top [genre] songs"

"Alexa, play the top songs by [artist]"

Discover new music

When you're tired of hearing the same old beats, here are some commands you can try...

"Alexa, play new music"

"Alexa, play more songs like this"

"Alexa, play the song of the day"

"Alexa, play songs I've never heard"

"Alexa, play songs similar to [artist]"

"Alexa, play new [genre] music"

"Alexa, play other music I like"

Learn about music

If you hear a wonderful track and want to find out more, then here's what to say...

"Alexa, who is this by?"

"Alexa, who sings this song?"

"Alexa, who's in this band?"

"Alexa, what year did this [song or album] come out?"

"Alexa, tell me more about this song"

Adjust audio settings

Some of the more expensive Alexa devices (such as the Echo and Echo Studio) include multiple speakers that can fill an entire room with audio. If you find that the high and low tones don't sound quite right in your room, then it's possible to adjust three settings...

Bass

By adjusting the bass, you can control the lowest frequencies in music. Typically the higher the bass, the more rumble you feel.

Treble

This controls the highest frequencies and tones in music.

Midrange

This controls all of the frequencies and tones that lie in between the bass and treble. By increasing this, you can often hear the instrumentals better.

To adjust any of these settings, use the following commands..

"Alexa, increase the bass"

"Alexa, increase the treble"

"Alexa, increase the midrange"

"Alexa, decrease the bass"

"Alexa, decrease the treble"

"Alexa, decrease the midrange"

"Alexa, set the bass to maximum"

"Alexa, set the treble to maximum"

"Alexa, set the midrange to maximum"

"Alexa, reset the equaliser"

"Alexa, set the [bass/treble/midrange] to [number from -6 to 6]

Tip! Use the touchscreen

If you have an Echo Show or Echo Spot, then it's possible to use the touchscreen to adjust audio settings. To do this, swipe downwards from the top of the screen, tap **Settings**, choose **Sounds**, tap **Equaliser**, then use the sliders.

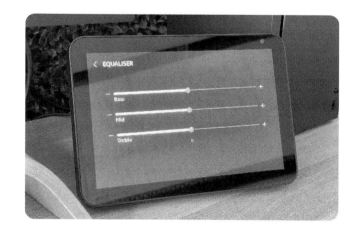

Listen to the radio

Listen to music the old way...

Your Alexa can do more than just play music. It can also play podcasts, audiobooks, or even radio stations - as we explore on this page.

There are two types of radio stations for Alexa. The first is traditional radio. By listening to these, you'll hear news stories, ads, DJs, and even traffic reports. For this to work, you'll need to use TuneIn, a streaming service that plays radio over the internet. TuneIn should be enabled by default, but if it isn't, please reference the "Music: set up your Alexa" chapter. The second type of stations available for Alexa are playlist stations. These are stations based around artists, genres, or eras. There are no ads if you're subscribed to Amazon Music Unlimited - just continuous music.

Radio commands

Hear's what you need to say to load a radio station...

"Alexa, play [station name]"

"Alexa, play radio station [name]"

"Alexa, play radio station [frequency]"

"Alexa, play radio station [genre]"

"Alexa, play radio station [era]"

"Alexa, play radio station [artist]"

Browse radio stations from your phone

You don't have to use voice commands to start radio stations, because you can also use the Alexa app to browse stations and then play them through your Alexa device. Here's how it works:

1. Open the Alexa app on your phone or tablet. Tap **Play**, look for **TUNEIN LOCAL RADIO**, then tap the **Browse** button.

2. Search for a station, or browse through the stations on display.

3. Tap on a station, then choose your Alexa to start listening.

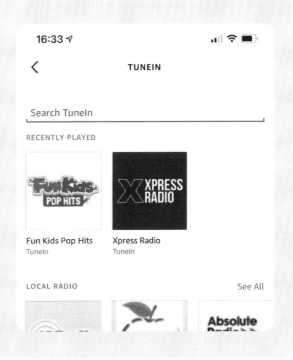

Explore the Amazon Music app

Listen to music and podcasts on your phone or tablet...

While Alexa is a fantastic way to explore and listen to music within your home, you can also jam to the same tunes via the Amazon Music app, which is available for the iPhone, iPad, and Android smartphones. It's a fantastic way to explore music, with helpful suggestions based on your listening history, and an intuitive home screen that presents the latest albums, playlists, and stations.

To find the Amazon Music app, open the App Store on your device and search for "Amazon Music".

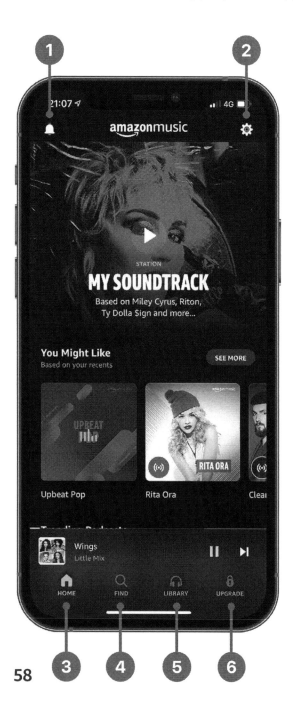

Exploring the Amazon Music app

Here's a quick overview of the Amazon Music app on a smartphone:

1. Tap **activity** to see updates from any artists you follow.

2. Tap on the **Settings** button to adjust streaming quality, enable Car Mode, access help, and more.

3. Return to the Home screen of Amazon Music.

4. Search for music and podcasts by tapping this button. You'll also see shortcuts to genres of music, stations, charts, and new releases.

5. Any albums, artists, playlists, and songs you've saved from Amazon Music will appear here.

6. Amazon Music is a free service with regular adverts placed inbetween songs. By tapping here you can upgrade to Amazon Music Unlimted, which enables Alexa, removes ads, and lets you download music so you can listen offline.

Download music

While browsing songs, albums, or playlists, tap the **download** button (it looks like an arrow pointing down), to save the music to your device. You can now listen to it offline.

Add music to your Library

You can add music to your Library by tapping the **plus** button. To explore your music library, tap the **Library** button at the bottom of the screen.

See information about music

While listening to music, tap on the thumbnail at the bottom of the screen, then tap the **X-Ray** button. You'll now see interesting information about the music and its artist.

Enable Alexa

If you have subscribed to Amazon Music Unlimited, you'll see a button in the bottom-right corner for enabling Alexa. To use Alexa, just tap this button and say a command out loud.

Switch to Car Mode

Car Mode simplifies the interface of Amazon Music, making it easier to control playback or access Alexa. To enable Car Mode, tap the **Settings** button, then **Car Mode**.

Create a playlist

While viewing an album or song, tap the **options** button to its right, then tap **Add to Playlist**. You can now choose from your existing playlists, or create a new one.

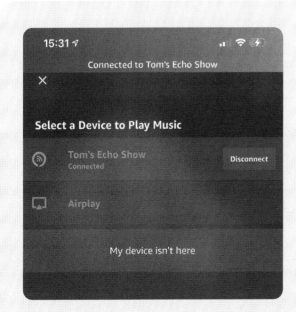

Play music through your Alexa

If your phone and Alexa device are connected to the same Wi-Fi network, then it's possible to play music through your Alexa speakers. To do this:

1. Tap the **Settings** button in the top-right corner.

2. Tap **Connect to a Device**.

3. The app will display a list of available devices. Tap on your Alexa, and the Amazon Music app will now play through its speakers.

Listen to audiobooks

Enjoy a lengthy book while doing other tasks...

Reading a great book is one of the most rewarding ways to spend a rainy afternoon, but there are times when it's not exactly convenient, like when you're exercising, driving, or cooking a meal. That's where audiobooks come in. They're a more flexible way to enjoy a book, and if you're lucky, you might even get to hear the author read their work out loud.

Fortunately, the Alexa is a fantastic way to listen to audiobooks. By default, it uses Audible, a service owned and operated by Amazon. This means you can purchase an audiobook on Amazon (or at www.audible.com) and then ask Alexa to start playing it. You can also explore audiobooks using the Alexa app on your smartphone or tablet. Here's how it works...

Audiobook commands

After purchasing an audiobook via Amazon or Audible, here are some commands to get you going...

"Alexa, read [title]"

"Alexa, play [title] on Audible"

"Alexa, play the book [title]"

"Alexa, play audiobook [title]"

If you have an Echo Show:
"Alexa, show me my audiobooks"

Audiobook playback commands

While listening to an audiobook, here's how you can control the playback...

"Alexa, pause"

"Alexa, resume"

"Alexa, resume my book"

To rewind 30 seconds:
"Alexa, go back"

To go forward 30 seconds:
"Alexa, go forward"

To restart the chapter:
"Alexa, restart"

"Alexa, next chapter"

"Alexa, previous chapter"

"Alexa, go to chapter [number]"

Find new audiobooks at Audible

Audible is the best place to find new audiobooks. It has the world's largest selection of audiobooks and podcasts, and because it's tied to your Amazon account, anything you purchase can be played over your Alexa device. Here's how to use Audible:

Visit the Audible website

Go to **www.audible.com**, then use your Amazon account to log in. If you've never used Audible before then you'll be able to sign up for a 30-day trial.

Explore Audible

After logging in, use the **Browse** shortcut at the top of the screen to explore audiobooks and podcasts.

Purchase titles

After finding a suitable audiobook or podcast, click the **Buy** button to purchase it and place it into your library. You can now play it on your Alexa by saying "Alexa, play audiobook [title]" out loud.

Listen to Kindle eBooks

Let Alexa read a book to you...

As we discovered on the previous two pages, listening to audiobooks is a great way to hear a book read aloud by a professional speaker, actor, or author. Alas, not every book is available as an audiobook, but help is at hand, as Alexa can read a Kindle book to you over its speakers. It's not as effective as a human (it can often be monotone and lack any sense of humour), but if you have a wide selection of eBooks in your account, then it's at least worth a try.

Kindle commands

To ask Alexa to read a Kindle book out loud, just say...

"Alexa, read [title] on Kindle"

"Alexa, read [title]"

"Alexa, read the book [title]"

If you have an Echo Show:
"Alexa, show me my Kindle book [title]"

Kindle playback commands

Just like controlling an audiobook, you can say the following to control playback of a Kindle book...

"Alexa, pause"

"Alexa, resume"

"Alexa, resume my book"

To rewind 30 seconds:
"Alexa, go back"

To go forward 30 seconds:
"Alexa, go forward"

To restart the chapter:
"Alexa, restart"

"Alexa, next chapter"

"Alexa, previous chapter"

"Alexa, go to chapter [number]"

Stream audio from your smartphone or tablet

Play music over Bluetooth through your Alexa...

It's highly likely that your Alexa has much better speakers than your smartphone or tablet, especially if you have the high-end Echo Studio, which has five incredible speakers that can fill a room with audio. If so, then it's a good idea to stream audio from your smartphone directly through Alexa's speakers. There are many ways to do this, but the simplest is to connect your smartphone and Alexa via Bluetooth.

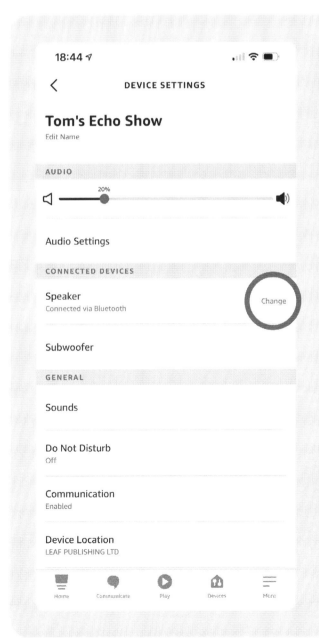

Stream music over Bluetooth

1. Open the Alexa app on your smartphone, then tap **Devices** at the bottom of the screen.

2. Tap on the Alexa device you wish to stream audio to.

3. Look for the Speaker section. If it says "Built-in speaker", tap the **Change** button to its right.

4. Tap **Bluetooth**, then **Pair a New Device**. Your Alexa is now in Pairing Mode, which means it is scanning the area for Bluetooth devices.

5. On your smartphone or tablet, open its Bluetooth settings. If you're using an Apple device, open the **Settings** app, tap **Bluetooth**, and make sure Bluetooth is turned on. On an Android device, go to **Settings** > **Connections** > **Bluetooth** and make sure Bluetooth is turned on.

6. Wait a short while, and look for your Alexa to appear in the Bluetooth devices panel. Once it does, tap on it to connect your smartphone and Alexa. Now, any audio you play on your smartphone will be streamed to your Alexa and played through its speakers.

Watch Amazon Prime

Watch movies, TV shows, and more on your Echo Show...

With an Echo Show and an Amazon Prime account, you can watch thousands of movies, TV shows, and original content on Amazon Prime. Anything you watch is streamed at 540p (not HD, but pretty close), which looks great on the touchscreen, and with the audio turned up, you have a fully-fledged miniature TV in your room. To open Amazon Prime on your Echo, say:

"Alexa, open Amazon Prime"

You'll then see Amazon Prime open on your Echo. Next, use the touchscreen to browse through content, or use the following commands to find videos:

"Alexa, play [TV or movie title]"

"Alexa, show me [category or genre] on Amazon Prime"

"Alexa, show me new movies"

"Alexa, show me new TV shows"

"Alexa, show me films starring [name] on Amazon Prime"

"Alexa, show me films directed by [name] on Amazon Prime"

"Alexa, search for [keyword] on Amazon Prime"

"Alexa, show me my video library"

"Alexa, show me my watchlist"

Playback commands

While watching content on Amazon Prime, you can use the following commands to control playback:

"Alexa, pause"

"Alexa, resume"

"Alexa, rewind" (rewinds 10 seconds)

"Alexa, fast-forward" (jumps 10 seconds ahead)

"Alexa, next episode"

"Alexa, previous episode"

Watch Netflix

Access Neflix on your Echo Show...

If you've seen everything on Amazon Prime, then it's time to jump over to Netflix, where you'll find millions of hours of movies, TV shows, and original content. It works surprisingly well on the Echo Show, with punchy audio and video content streamed at 540p. To start watching content on Netflix, say:

"Alexa, open Netflix"

You'll then see the Netflix app open on your Echo. Next, use the touchscreen to enter your Netflix account details. Once logged in, use the touchscreen to browse through content, or use the following commands to find videos:

"Alexa, play [title] on Netflix"

"Alexa, show me [category or genre] on Netflix"

"Alexa, show me films starring [name] on Netflix"

"Alexa, show me films directed by [name] on Netflix"

"Alexa, search for [keyword] on Netflix"

While watching content on Netflix, you can use the same commands on the previous page to control playback.

Watch videos on the web

Stream content from YouTube, Vimeo, and more...

Amazon Prime and Netflix are great for watching TV shows and movies, but if you want to entertain your cat with bird videos, then YouTube is a much better option. Your Echo Show or Spot can search the web for videos relating to subjects you specify. It will use the Bing search engine to look through YouTube, Vimeo, and Dailymotion, then show any relevant results.

Search for videos

When you're ready to search the web for videos, say:

"Alexa, show me [subject] videos"   "Alexa, show me videos""

Alexa will then display a carousel of videos it found. You can swipe through them with your finger, then tap on one to watch it. While watching a video, you can jump to the next one by swiping left across the screen. Similarly, to go back to the previous video, swipe right.

Playback commands

While watching videos on the web, you can use the following commands to control playback:

"Alexa, pause"   "Alexa, previous video"

"Alexa, resume"   "Alexa, full-screen"

"Alexa, next video"

Take a photo or video

Capture a photo or video of yourself using the Echo Spot or Show camera...

Both the Echo Spot and the Echo Show come with a forward-facing camera, which means you can make video calls or take a photo of yourself. Any images you capture are stored online in your Photo Booth, which is part of Amazon Photos. If you have a basic Amazon account, then you're able to store 5GB worth of images. There's no limit, however, if you have Amazon Prime.

Take a photo

When you're ready to capture a photo of yourself, say:

"Alexa, take a photo"   "Alexa, take a picture"

You'll then see a three-second countdown appear on-screen. Strike a pose, or swipe to the left to apply one of several stickers (including a moustache and pair of glasses). When the countdown finishes, Alexa will capture a photo and save it to your Photo Booth.

Capture a video

To record a video of yourself using the front-facing camera, say:

"Alexa, take a video"   "Alexa, record me"

Once the recording begins, you'll see a red button appear at the bottom of the screen. You can tap this to end the video or say "*Alexa, stop*".

View your photos and videos

To view your photos or videos, say:

"Alexa, show me my photos"   "Alexa, previous"

To control playback: "Alexa, resume"

"Alexa, next"   "Alexa, stop"

Chapter 05

Communication

What's the first thing that comes to mind when you think about Alexa? I'm willing to bet a considerable sum that it's *not* making phone calls. Nor sending text messages, or making video calls, or even dropping in on other Echo devices; but that's exactly what Alexa can do. All of these features are free to use and surprisingly easy to perform. This chapter will cover all of this, enabling you to turn your Echo into a fully-fledged communications device in no time.

In this chapter:

An introduction to communication

Make calls, send messages and more...

You probably think of Alexa as a helpful assistant, one that's able to quickly answer questions and play music; but there's a side of Alexa you might not know about, and it's all about communication with other human beings. Yes, that's right, your Alexa can make phone calls, video calls, send text messages, and even drop in on other Alexa devices. Over the next few pages we'll explore each of these, but for now here's a quick overview:

Voice calls

With Alexa-to-Alexa, you can make phone calls to other Alexa devices. You can also call mobile phones using the Alexa-to-mobile feature, and even call landlines (if you're in the US, Canada, or Mexico) using Alexa-to-Landland Calling feature.

Video calls

If you have an Echo Spot or Show, then you can make free video calls to other Alexa devices with a screen.

Text messages

If you know someone who also has an Alexa, then you can send them free text messages, which appear on their Alexa Spot or Show.

Drop In

Think of Drop In as an intercom system that works between Alexa devices. This means that if you have multiple Alexa devices within your home, you can drop in on the Alexa in your kitchen with just a simple commands. You can also drop in on any contacts with Alexa Drop In enabled on their device.

All of these communication features are free to use, but there might be limitations depending on your location and device.

Add your contacts

Tell Alexa who your friends and family members are...

Alexa is pretty smart and can dial a number that you request, but if you ask it to call "Bob" or your best friend from high school, then it won't know what to do. Not unless you've added all of your contacts to the Alexa app. Once you've done that, Alexa will know exactly who Bob is, who your plumber is, or even your second best friend from high school.

One thing to keep in mind is that Alexa categories your contacts into two groups:

Alexa-to-Alexa contacts

These are people in your contacts list who also have an Alexa device. You can send a text message to these people, drop in on their device, and if you both have an Alexa with video support - make video calls.

Non-Alexa contacts

These are people in your contacts list who don't have an Alexa device. You can still call these people, but you can't send text messages or make video calls.

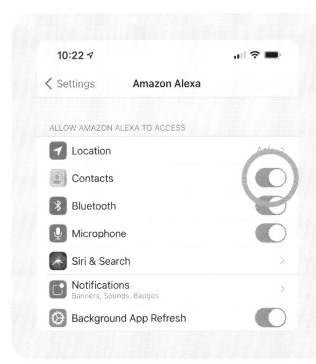

How to add your contacts to Alexa

Chances are, you already have all of your friends and family members set up on your smartphone. You can quickly add them to the Alexa app on your phone, which instantly lets Alexa know who's who.

1. **If using an iPhone:** Open the **Settings** app, scroll down, then tap **Amazon Alexa**. Next, make sure the **Contacts** toggle is turned on.

2. **If using an Android phone:** Open **Settings**, tap **Apps**, then tap **Amazon Alexa**. Look for **Permissions**, then make sure **Contacts** is turned on.

Add a nickname to a contact

When you decide to get in touch with someone using Alexa, you'll need to say something like, "Alexa, call Bob". This works great if your contact has a short name, but if they have a first and last name, or there are multiple "Bobs", it can soon become a chore having to state their name in full or remember which is Bob 1 and which is Bob 2.

To help, you can assign a nickname to someone, then use it to get in touch with them. To do this:

1. Open the Alexa app, tap **Communicate**, then tap the **group** icon in the top-right corner.

2. Tap the contact you wish to assign a nickname.

3. Tap the **Add Nickname**.

4. Enter a nickname for the contact, then tap **Save**.

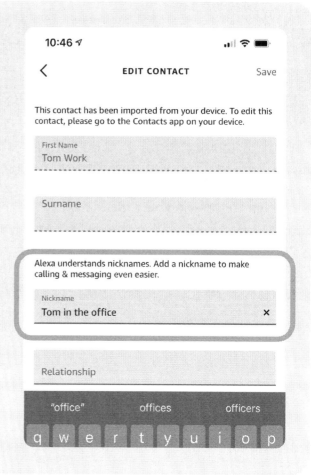

Block someone

If someone is continuously spamming your Alexa with annoying phone calls, video calls, and messages, then you can block them from getting in touch. To do this:

1. Open the Alexa app, tap **Communicate**, then tap the **group** icon in the top-right corner.

2. Tap the **options** button in the top-right corner of the Contacts list. It looks like three dots stacked on top of each other.

3. Tap **Block Contacts**.

4. If you know the person's name, tap **Block by Contact Name** to look through your contacts list, then tap Block.

5. If you only have the phone number for the person you wish to block, tap **Block by Phone Number**, then enter the number you wish to block.

72

Make a voice call

Call other Alexa's, mobiles, or even landlines...

With it's punchy speakers and powerful microphone, the Alexa makes for a surprisingly great phone calling device. It's versatile too, letting you call other Alexa devices or mobile phones. Calls are free, but there are some limitations:

- You can't call the emergency services, such as 911 or 999.
- You can't call service numbers, like 311 or 411.
- You can't call premium-rate numbers.
- You can't dial letter numbers, like 1-500-AMAZON

Call another Alexa

When you're ready to call someone with an Alexa device, say:

"Alexa, call [name]"   "Alexa, phone [name]"

"Alexa, call [device]"   "Alexa, ring [name]"

Note that [device] refers to the name of another Alexa device on your Wi-Fi network, and [name] refers to the person's name or nickname if that person is in your contacts list.

Call someone you know

To call someone in your contacts list, say:

"Alexa, call [name]'s [label]"   "Alexa, phone [name]'s [label]"

Note that [label] refers to any labels you have added to contacts, for example a label might be their mobile, their home phone, or their work number.

Call a phone number

If you know the phone number you wish to call, say:

"Alexa, call [phone number]"   "Alexa, dial [phone number]"

Answer a call

If someone you know tries to get in touch via your Alexa, then you have two ways to answer:

Alexa devices without a screen

When a call comes through, your Alexa will flash a green ring, you'll hear a tone, and Alexa will say, "*[name] would like to talk*". Say "*Answer*" to begin a phone call, or say "*Ignore*" if you don't want to talk.

Alexa devices with a screen

If you have an Echo Spot or Show, then you'll hear a tone; Alexa will say "*[name] would like to talk*", and you'll see buttons for answering or declining the call. To answer, tap the green **Answer** button or say "*Answer*". To ignore, tap the **Decline** button or say "*Ignore*".

End a call

When you're ready to hang up, say:

"Alexa, hang up"   "Alexa, end call"

If you're using an Echo Spot or Show, then you can also press the red **End** button on the screen.

Make a video call

Chat face to face using an Echo Spot or Show...

If you're lucky enough to own an Echo Spot or Show, and know someone else with a video-based Alexa, then it's possible to give them a video call and talk face to face, totally free. Here's how it works:

Video call commands

When you're ready to video call someone, say:

"Alexa, video call [name]"   "Alexa, video call [device]"

Video call controls

Mute your audio: Tap on the screen then tap the MUTE button.

Turn off your video: Tap on the screen then tap the VIDEO OFF button.

Move the thumbnail: Simply slide it to another corner of the screen.

Adjust the brightness: Swipe down from the top of the screen, then use the Brightness slider.

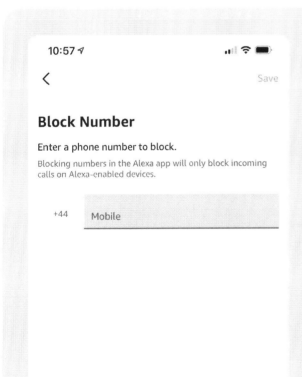

Make a group video call

It's possible to talk to up to seven people at once during a video call. To do this, you'll need to create a group of contacts using the Alexa app on your smartphone, then start a video call with the entire group. Here's how it works:

1. Open the Alexa app, tap **Communicate**, then tap the **group** icon in the top-right corner.

2. Tap **Add New**, then choose **Add Group**. If you're asked to enabling Group Calling, tap **Enable**.

3. Scroll through your contacts and tick the people you wish to add to the group.

4. Give the group a name, then tap **Create Group**.

5. To start a video call with the group, say "*Alexa, call [group name]*.

Send a text message

Send a message and have Alexa read it out loud...

If you're not comfortable with making voice and video calls, then it's possible to send a text message, which the recipient can read on their Echo Spot or Show screen, or ask Alexa to read out loud. Sending text messages via Alexa will only work if both you and the recipient have either an Alexa device or the Alexa app installed, so you can't send SMS messages to regular phones.

Text messaging commands

When you're ready to text someone, say:

"Alexa, send a text message"   "Alexa, send a message"

Alexa will respond by saying, "To whom?". Next, say:

"[name]"

Alexa will respond by saying, "*Did you mean [name]?*". You can confirm or reject by saying:

"Yes"   "No"

If correct, Alexa will say, "*What's the message?*" You can then recite the message out loud. When you're finished, Alexa will say, "*Got it. Should I sent it?*" You can then confirm by saying:

"Yes"

Send a text message using the Alexa app

It's much quicker to have a message conversation with someone by using the Alexa app, as you can type or even record messages in real time - rather than talk to Alexa. To send messages via the Alexa app:

1 Open the Alexa app, tap **Communicate**, then tap the **Message** button.

2 Select a contact, and the Alexa app will open a conversation window.

3 Type your message using the text box at the bottom of the screen. Alternatively, you can record a voice message by tapping the **microphone** button.

4 Tap the **arrow** button when you're ready to send your message.

Recieving a text message

When someone sends you a message through Alexa, one of several things will happen:

- You'll hear a tone on your Alexa device.

- If your Alexa has a display, a notification will appear at the top of the screen that says "Message for [you] from [name]". After the notification goes away, a small message bubble will be shown in the top-right corner.

- If your Alexa doesn't have a screen, you'll see a yellow ring pulsate.

- On a smartphone with the Alexa app installed, you'll see a standard notification to let you know that a message has arrived.

Drop In on another Alexa

Talk to someone in another room of the house...

If you have multiple Alexa's scattered throughout the house, then it's possible to "Drop In" on other Alexa devices that are sharing the same Wi-Fi connection. It works a little like a walkie talkie, enabling you to have a voice or video conversation in between rooms. You can also drop in on someone's smartphone if they have the Alexa app installed.

It's worth noting that people can only drop in on your device or smartphone if you give them permission to do so, so don't worry about strangers suddenly talking at you through your Alexa.

Enable Drop In on your smartphone

To let people in your home drop in on your smartphone, open the Alexa app and:

1 Tap **Communicate**, then tap the **Drop In** button at the top of the screen.

2 If you haven't enabled Drop In yet, then a pop-up window will appear asking you to turn it on. If this doesn't appear, tap on the **group** profile button in the top-right corner, then tap **My Communication Settings** underneath your profile. Next, toggle **Allow Drop In** on.

Let a contact Drop In

To give someone permission to Drop In on your Alexa, grab your smartphone and open the Alexa app.

1 Tap **Communicate**, then tap the **group** profile button in the top-right corner to show your contacts list.

2 Select the contact you want to allow.

3 Toggle **Allow Drop In** on. When the app asks you to confirm, tap **Yes**.

Drop In commands

When you're ready to drop in on another Alexa device, say:

"Alexa, drop in on [name]"   "Alexa, drop in on [device]"

Note that [name] refers to the person's name or nickname added to contacts. [device] refers to the name of the Alexa device on your network. It might be "Echo Show", "Echo Dot", or a name you've specified in the Alexa app.

Drop In announcement

If you have multiple Alexa's scattered throughout the house and need to get the attention of everyone at once (say, for example, dinner is ready), then you can perform an Alexa Announcement. When this happens, your voice will be boomed simultaneously out of every Alexa device at once. It's a great way to get everyone's attention. To perform an Alexa announcement, say:

"Alexa, announce [message]"   "Alexa, broadcast [message]"

Chapter 06

Shopping and information

When you think of Amazon, you probably imagine a giant warehouse where nearly anything is available to purchase. You wouldn't be far off, as behind the scenes, Amazon uses hundreds of warehouses and distribution centres to ship products to customers around the world.

Of course, selling and shipping products isn't Amazon's only source of revenue. It also powers more than half the internet (yes, really), streams TV shows and movies over Amazon Prime, creates its own computer hardware, and powers Alexa; so it only makes sense that you can use Alexa to browse and buy things from Amazon. This chapter takes a look at how you can purchase products on Amazon, then explores the many ways you can get information on the world around you.

In this chapter:

Buy things on Amazon

Find products and purchase them with your voice...

If you didn't already know, Amazon is an online store where you can buy literally anything you can think of. Over the last couple of decades, it has become so successful that it has now become the biggest and most successful retailer in history, so it makes sense that you can purchase items from the Amazon website using its most popular voice assistant: Alexa.

Before you can purchase items from Amazon using your voice, you'll need to make sure Voice Purchasing is enabled on your Alexa. It *should* be enabled by default, but in case you want to double-check:

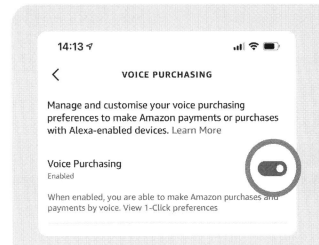

Enable Voice Purchasing on your smartphone

1 Open the Alexa app on your phone, tap the **More** button, then choose **Settings**.

2 Tap **Account Settings**, then **Voice Purchasing**.

3 If Voice Purchasing isn't enabled, toggle the switch on.

You will also need the following things set up on your Amazon account:

- A valid payment method and shipping address.

- 1-Click Purchasing enabled. If you're unsure, head over to the Amazon website, log in, then go to your account settings. From there select **1-Click settings** and make sure it's not disabled.

- An active Amazon Prime account. To sign up for Amazon Prime, visit the Amazon website, log in, then go to your account settings. On the following webpage you'll see a shortcut to Amazon Prime in the upper-right corner.

Find products on Amazon

Now that you're set up to purchase items over Alexa, it's time to start exploring the millions of products available on Amazon. If you're feeling unsure as to which exact product is the best choice available, then you can ask Alexa for product recommendations. These are based on customer reviews, ratings, and sales rankings. To get a product recommendation, say:

"Alexa, recommend me a [product]"

"Alexa, find the best [product]"

"Alexa, find the most popular [product]"

"Alexa, what's the best selling [product]?"

"Alexa, what's the highest-rated [product]

Note that [product] refers to the name or category of products you wish to buy. After your request, Alexa will respond with a product name, user rating, number of reviews, and price. If you have an Echo Spot or Show, then you'll also see a gallery of items on the display.

Order a product on Amazon

If you know which product you would like to buy on Amazon, say:

"Alexa, buy [item]"

"Alexa, order [item]"

"Alexa, purchase [item]"

If you have an Echo Spot or Show, then you'll see a gallery of products appear on the screen. Tap on one to see more information, add it to your basket, or purchase straight away.

If you have an Echo, Echo Dot, or Echo Auto, then Alexa will tell you about the item it has found, then say, *"Do you want to buy it?"*. Say *"Yes"* to order the product straight away.

Order multiple products

If you'd like to order more than one of a particular product, just say:

"Alexa, buy [quantity] of [item]"

"Alexa, order [quantity] of [item]"

"Alexa, purchase [quantity] of [item]"

For quantity, state the number of items you wish to purchase. Keep in mind that you can't order multiple different items, just quantities of a single item.

Reorder a product

If you've purchased something before on Amazon then it's super easy to reorder it, just say:

"Alexa, reorder [item]"   "Alexa, order [item] again"

Alexa will look through your order history to try and find the exact item. If it finds it, then Alexa will say, "*Do you want to buy it?*". Say "*Yes*" to confirm.

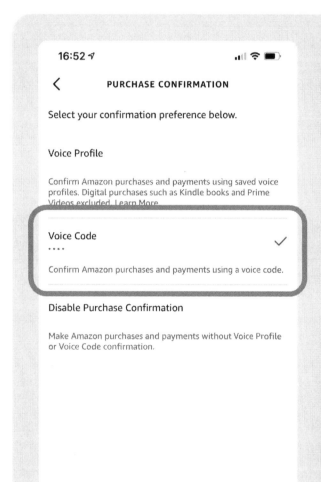

Enable Voice Code for purchases

Alexa is great at recognising words, but it can't recognise individuals and their voices. This means anyone can order a product (or multiple products) using your Alexa, and you'll have to foot the bill. To prevent this from happening, you can enable a Voice Code for purchases, which means anyone that tries to purchase something will need to confirm with a four-digit code. To enable this:

1 Open the Alexa app on your phone, tap the **More** button, then choose **Settings**.

2 Tap **Account Settings**, then choose **Voice Purchasing**.

3 Look for *Purchase Confirmation*, then tap the **Manage** link to its right.

4 Tap **Voice Code**.

5 Enter a four-digit code, then tap **Save**.

Now, when you place an order using Alexa, you'll be asked for your four-digit code before the purchase is confirmed.

Check a delivery status

If you've ordered something from Amazon, and want to find out where your delivery is, say

"Alexa, where's my stuff?"

Alexa will look for the delivery status, then let you know the when it is expected to arrive.

Turn on delivery notifications

On its default setting, Alexa will let you know when an item is out for delivery, but not when it has been delivered. You can change this and then receive notifications when an item is on its way. To do this:

1. Open the Alexa app on your smartphone, tap **More**, then **Settings**.

2. Next, tap **Notifications**, then **Amazon Shopping**.

3. To receive a notification when an item is out for delivery, make sure **Out for delivery** is toggled on.

4. To receive a notification when an item has been delivered, toggle **Delivered** on.

5. If you want to know when gifts are out for delivery and then delivered, toggle the second switch from the top on.

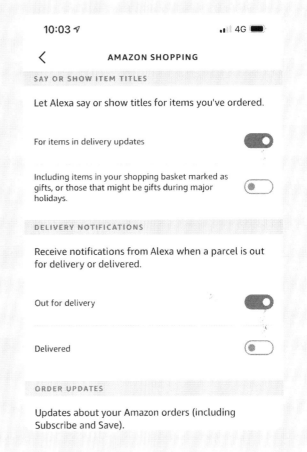

Get the latest news

Listen to Alexa's Flash Briefing...

Think of Alexa's Flash Briefing as a quick update on the latest news, as well as any content that you've added using the Alexa app. They're usually around two to three minutes long (although some are up to 10 minutes), which means you can quickly get informed on a number of topics before you start your day. To hear your Flash Briefing, just say either of these:

"Alexa, play my Flash Briefing"   "Alexa, give me the news"

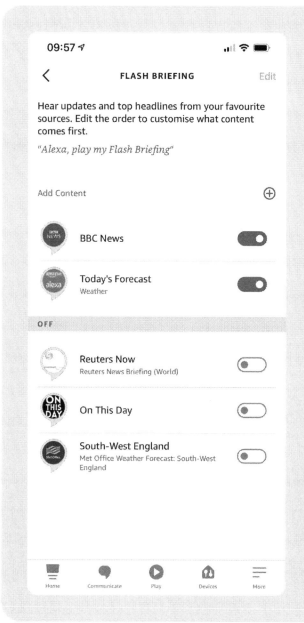

Customise your Flash Briefing

While the default Flash Briefing is pretty great at giving you an overview of the latest news and events, you can customise it with literally thousands of briefing options. They include local news stations, insider news, specific categories of information, and much more. Here's how it works:

1. Open the Alexa app on your phone, tap the **More** button, then choose **Settings**.

2. Scroll down, then tap **Flash Briefing**.

3. The app will display several skills that are available for you to use. Tap on one to see a brief description, user reviews, and the average user rating.

4. To add the skill to your Flash Briefing, tap **Enable to Use**.

5. Tap the **back arrow** to return to the Flash Briefing overview.

6. Repeat the steps above to explore and add additional Flash Briefing skills.

7. From the overview screen, you can also enable and disable Flash Briefing skills by toggling them on or off.

Control Flash Briefings

If you're not interested in a Flash Briefing, say:

"Alexa, next"   "Alexa, stop"

Re-order Flash Briefings

It's easy to re-order your Flash Briefings:

1. Open the Alexa app on your phone, tap the **More** button, then choose **Settings**.

2. Scroll down, then tap **Flash Briefing**.

3. Tap the **Edit** button in the top-right corner.

4. Tap and hold on a Flash Briefing, then slide it up or down to re-order it.

5. Tap **Done** when you're finished.

A few Flash Briefing highlights:

Here are a few recommended Flash Briefings to start your day:

 Reuters
If you just want the facts, then the Reuters Flash Briefing gets straight to the point. If you have an Echo Show, then you'll also see it as a video Flash Briefing.

 Everyday Positivity Flash Briefing
Hosted by Kate Cocker, you'll hear a daily piece of positivity to help lift your day and put you in the right state of mind to thrive.

 Weather
If you haven't already guessed, this Flash Briefing will give you an overview of the weather conditions in your local area.

 Weird AF News
Listen to off-beat stories, strange history, the paranormal, and other humourous news. This is one Flash Briefing that will always make you smile.

Get the weather forecast

If you're planning a day out, ask Alexa for the weather...

Depending on where you live, the weather can dramatically change from day to day, or even hour to hour. Alexa is pretty good at guessing the conditions ahead, so to get a weather forecast for your area, try asking one of these commands:

"Alexa, what's the weather like?"

"Alexa, how's the weather"

"Alexa, what's the weather like in [location]?"

"Alexa, what's the temperature?"

"Alexa, is it raining?"

"Alexa, do I need an umbrella?"

"Alexa, is it windy?"

Get more detailed weather reports

When you ask some weather commands (such as the first two listed above), Alexa will go into more detail about the weather outside. For specific information about the forecast, you can also ask these commands:

"Alexa, what's the extended weather forecast?"

"Alexa, what will the weather be like at [time]?"

"Alexa, what will the weather be like on [day]?"

"Alexa, will it rain on [day]?"

"Alexa, will it snow on [day]?"

Get traffic conditions

Find out of you'll make it to work on time...

If you're worried about arriving late at work or have a long journey planned, then it's a good idea to get an overview of the traffic conditions ahead. If you're wondering how Alexa knows where you work or want to go, don't worry because it's not listening or trying to guess. Instead, you can use the Alexa app on your smartphone to set a start and endpoint (and even a stop along the way if necessary). This might sound like a longwinded way to get traffic conditions, but if you regularly travel back and forth to the same place, then you can set the start and endpoint once, then get traffic conditions for the same route each day.

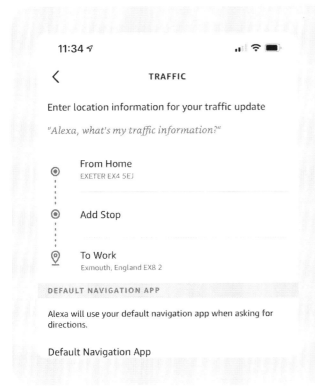

Set a start and end point for traffic conditions

Grab your smartphone and open the Alexa app, then...

1. Tap the **More** button and choose **Settings**.

2. Scroll down, then tap **Traffic**.

3. The Traffic screen appears. You should see your Home address already inputted, but you can change this by tapping **From Home**.

4. To add a stop along the way, tap **Add Stop**, enter an address, then tap **Save**.

5. To add an endpoint, tap **To Work**, enter an address, then tap **Save**.

Ask for traffic conditions

Now that you have your home and endpoint saved, you can get the traffic conditions by saying:

"Alexa, how's traffic?"   "Alexa, what's my commute like?"

Alexa will then respond by giving you an estimated journey time, with suggested routes to take.

Chapter 07

Lists, alerts, and calendar

Unlike traditional desktop computers, some of the more popular locations to place Alexa include the kitchen and living room. These are areas where you might be performing a task (such as cooking), and need to set a timer, make a list, or remind yourself to do something in the near future. Thankfully, Alexa is great for performing all of these actions, able to set a timer or add items to just with just a simple command.

In this chapter:

10:04
☀ 55°

12 PM 60°

3 PM 64°

6 PM 62°

Taylor's Birthday
Today at 8:00 AM

"Show my calendar"

amazon music

Ask Me Anything
Neil Frances

Create Lists

Add, edit, and manage lists and or to-dos...

It's easy to forget something. Maybe you have to feed the neighbours cat, collect a child from school, or pick up some groceries on the way home. Whatever it is you need to remember, Alexa can help using lists. There are two types of list available:

Shopping

As you might imagine, these are lists of things or items that you'd like to purchase or keep track of. Alexa calls these Shopping lists, but you can make lists of anything you like.

To-Do

Think of a To-Do list as a set of reminders. You can add to-dos such as making coffee, hitting the gym, making an appointment, pretty much anything you can think of. You can check your to-do list at any time by asking Alexa or checking the app on your phone.

Create a list

When you're ready to create a list, say:

> "Alexa, create a list" "Alexa, create a list called [name]"

If you don't specify a name, then Alexa will ask for one. She will then ask for the first item.

Add, remove, and clear lists

If you already have a list set up, then you can say:

> "Alexa, add [item] to [list name]"
>
> "Alexa, check off [item] in my [list name]"
>
> "Alexa, remove [item] from [list name]"
>
> "Alexa, clear my [list name]"

If you have an Echo Spot or Show, then you can make things easier by saying, "Alexa, show me my [list name]". You'll then see the list of items on the Alexa display.

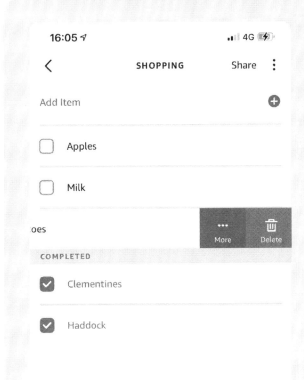

View your list using the Alexa app

While Alexa is great for making lists using your voice, it's not exactly efficient at reading back your list items. To make things easier, it's worth using the Alexa app on your smartphone to view lists and to-dos. You can also add, check, and remove items.

1. Open the Alexa app on your phone, tap the **More** button, then choose **Lists & Notes**.

2. The app will display shortcuts to your Shopping and To-Do lists. Tap on one to view the items within.

3. To add an item to a list, tap the blue **plus** button in the upper-right corner.

4. Tap on an item to mark it as complete.

5. To edit an item, tap on it, then use the on-screen keyboard.

6. To delete an item, swipe your finger from right to left, then tap **Delete**.

Create a reminder

Remind yourself to do something with Alexa Alerts...

Ever find yourself forgetting to do something? Alexa Alerts is here to help by reminding you to do things at set times. Let's say you need to take something out of the oven in 30 minutes; Alexa will make sure you don't forget. Need to set an alarm to wake you up in the morning? Alexa will make sure you don't sleep in.

Remind yourself to do something

When you want to set a new reminder, say:

"Alexa, set a reminder"

"Alexa, set a repeating reminder"

"Alexa, remind me to [task]"

"Alexa, remind me to [task] at [time]". For example, "Alexa, remind me to feed the cat at 6pm"

If you don't specifiy a task or time, then Alexa will ask you for those details.

Remind yourself of your reminders

If you've forgotten when your next reminder is, then say:

"Alexa, what's my next reminder?"

"Alexa, what are my reminders?"

If you have an Echo Spot or Show, then you can make things easier by saying, "Alexa, show me my [list name]". You'll then see the list of items on the Alexa display.

Cancel a reminder

If you no longer need to be reminded of somthing, say:

"Alexa, cancel my next reminder"

"Alexa, cancel all my reminders"

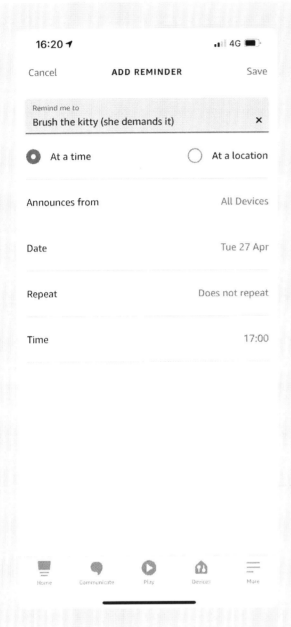

Use the Alexa app to create reminders

You might find it easier to create reminders using the Alexa app on your smartphone. To create a new reminder:

1 Open the Alexa app, tap the **More** button, then choose **Reminders**.

2 To create a new reminder, tap the **Add Reminder** button (or the **plus** button)

3 Use the **Remind me to** field to enter your reminder.

4 To be reminded at a specific time, make sure **At a time** is checked on.

5 If you have multiple Alexa's, the reminder will sound from all of them by default. To choose a specific Alexa, tap **All Devices**, then make a choice.

6 Use the **Date** option to pick a specific day for the reminder.

7 Use the **Repeat** option to set your reminder to repeat multiple times a day, every day, every week, month, or year.

8 Finally, use the **Time** field to set a time for your reminder.

9 Tap **Save**.

Set an alarm

Start the day with Alexa...

If you don't have a traditional bedside clock or prefer not to sleep next to your smartphone, then you can ask Alexa to wake you up at a specific time and date, and even with your favourite song.

Set an alarm

When you're ready to set an alarm, say:

"Alexa, set an alarm for [time]"

"Alexa, wake me up at [time]"

"Alexa, set a repeating alarm"

"Alexa, set a repeating alarm for [interval] at [time]". For example, "Alexa, set an alarm for every weekday at 8am"

If you forget to specifiy a time or date, then Alexa will ask you for the details.

Wake yourself with music

Alexa's default alarm sound isn't exactly inspiring, so if you'd rather wake to your favourite music, say:

"Alexa, wake me up to [song] at [time]"

"Alexa, wake me up to [genre] at [time]"

"Alexa, wake me up to [artist] at [time]"

"Alexa, wake me up to [playlist] at [time]"

Remind yourself of your next alarm

If you've forgotten when your next Alarm is, here's what to ask Alexa:

"Alexa, when is my next alarm?"

"Alexa, what are my alarms?"

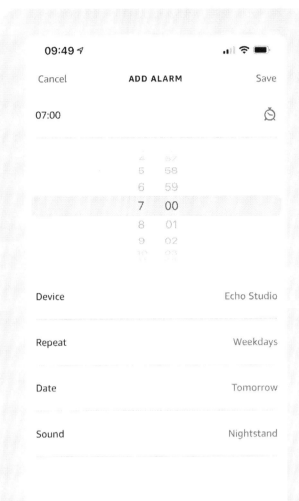

Use the Alexa app to set and edit alarms

You might find it easier to create reminders using the Alexa app on your smartphone. To create a new reminder:

1 Open the Alexa app, tap the **More** button, then choose **Alarms & Timers**.

2 To create a new alarm, tap either the large **plus** button or **Add Alarm**.

3 Use the vertical scrollers to pick a time.

4 If you have multiple Alexa's, the alarms will sound from all of them by default. To choose a specific Alexa, tap **Device**, then make a choice.

5 Use the **Repeat** option to set the alarm to ring every day, weekly, on every weekday, or at weekends.

6 Use the **Date** option to set the first alarm.

7 To choose an alarm sound, tap **Sound**, then pick from the many options available.

8 Tap **Save**.

What to do when Alexa wakes you up

When Alexa starts ringing the alarm, say either:

"Alexa, stop"   "Alexa, cancel"

You can also snooze for nine more minutes by saying:

"Alexa, snooze"

Set a timer

Perfect your timing with Alexa...

If you've ever tried to cook a complicated menu (like a roast), then you'll know how important a good countdown timer is. The chicken might take 120 minutes to cook, the roast potatoes 50, and the stuffing 25. That's before you factor in the vegetables, gravy, and the all-important dessert. If you have an Echo in the kitchen, then life is suddenly a lot easier because using Alexa, it's quickly possible to set a timer or even multiple timers, all running together.

Set a timer

To get your timer going, say:

"Alexa, set a timer"

"Alexa, create a timer for [duration]"

"Alexa, set a [name] timer"

"Alexa, set a [name] timer for [duration]". For example, "Alexa, set a chicken timer for 120 minutes"

If you forget to specifiy a duration, then Alexa will ask you for the details.

Get an update on your timer

If you need to know how long is left on the timer, say:

"Alexa, how long is left on my timer?"

"Alexa, what are my timers?"

"Alexa, how long is left on [name] timer?"

If you have an Alexa Spot or Show, then you can see your timer on the screen by saying "Alexa, show me my timer"

Delete timers

If you no longer need an upcoming timer, then say:

"Alexa, delete the timer"

"Alexa, delete the [name] timer"

"Alexa, delete all my timers"

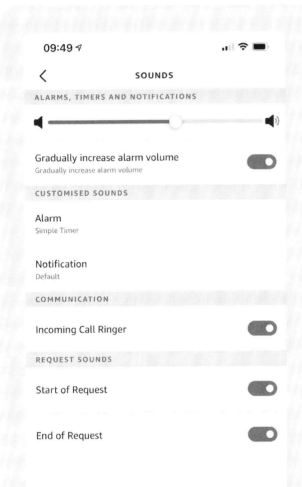

Manage alert and timer sound effects

When a timer or alert triggers, Alexa will play a simple sound effect using the volume your Echo is currently set to. This can be a startling way to wake up if your Alexa is set to a loud volume, so to customise the volume and pick another sound:

1. Open the Alexa app, tap the **Devices** button, and find the Echo device that you would like to customise.

2. Tap **Sounds**.

3. Use the slider near the top of the screen to adjust the volume level of alarms and timers.

4. If you want Alexa to slowly increase the volume of the timer or alarm, toggle **Gradually increase alarm volume** on.

5. To choose a different sound effect, tap **Alarm**. You can preview each sound effect by tapping on it then waiting a moment.

6. When you've finished making changes, tap the **back arrow** button in the top corner.

Add your calendar

Never miss an appointment or event with Alexa...

We all have busy lives with appointments to juggle, birthdays to remember, and events to attend. Alexa would be a pretty terrible assistant if it couldn't access and manage your calendar events, but thankfully it can. Once set up, it's possible to add events using just your voice, manage those events, and ask what's coming up. To get started, you'll need to use the Alexa app on your smartphone to connect Alexa to your calendar account. To do this:

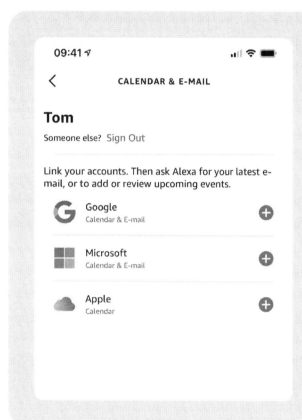

Link your calendar

Alexa can connect to a wide range of calendar account types, including Google, Apple, Office 365. To add one of these accounts:

1. Open the Alexa app, tap the **More** button, choose **Settings**, then tap **Calendar & Email.**

2. The app will display an overview of the calendar providers supported on your device.

3. Tap the **plus** button next to the calendar provider you use, then tap **Next.**

4. Follow the instructions to sign in to your account. If permissions are required to continue, follow the on-screen instructions.

5. Tap **Yes**, or **Allow**, when your calendar provider asks for permission to share your calendar with Alexa.

Add a calendar event

With your calendar account added to Alexa, you can now add an event by saying:

"Alexa, add an event to my calendar"

"Alexa, create an appointment"

"Alexa, add [event] to my calendar for [date] and [time]"

If you don't specify an event name, date, or time, then Alexa will ask for those details. One thing to note is that Alexa will create calendar events that last one hour. If you need to create an event that lasts longer (for example, an all-day event), then you'll need to do this using the calendar app on your smartphone or computer.

Add an event with someone you know

If you want to create a calendar event with someone in your Alexa Contacts list, say:

"Alexa, schedule [event] with [contact]"

"Alexa, create a meeting with [contact] called [event]"

See what's coming up on your calendar

If you have a busy day ahead and want to know what's next, say:

"Alexa, what's on my calendar today?"

"Alexa, what's on my calendar [day]?"

"Alexa, what's on my calendar [day] at [time]?"

Move or delete an event

If you need to make changes to the events in your calendar, say:

"Alexa, move my [event] to [time]"

"Alexa, move my [event] to [day]"

"Alexa, reschedule my [time] event to to [time]"

"Alexa, reschedule my [day] event to to [day]"

"Alexa, delete my [time] event"

"Alexa, cancel my [day] event"

"Alexa, delete [event] from my calendar"

Chapter 08

Skills and routines

Alexa is an incredibly powerful assistant, but by adding Skills to it you can unlock a nearly endless number of features. If you're wondering what skills are, think of them like apps for your smartphone. Some of them enable you to receive hour-by-hour weather forecast reports; some help you mediate, while others are fully-fledged computer games. If you're enjoying your time with Alexa and want to unlock even more features, then skills are the way to do it.

This chapter will explore skills, explain how to find them, and even tell you how to create your own original skills. It will also look at routines, which are chains of commands for Alexa that can be issued with just a single command. Don't worry if any of this sounds complicated, as it will all be explained in simple steps.

In this chapter:

Explore Skills and games

Give Alexa a new lease of life...

Alexa is amazing straight out of the box, able to understand nearly any command and almost instantly respond to it, and because Alexa is powered by the "cloud", it gets updated with new features on a regular basis. In many ways, Alexa is like the smartphone in your pocket: fantastic straight out of the box and updated regularly with new features. There's another similarity that Alexa shares with your smartphone: skills.

To get a better understanding of what a skill is, think of them like the apps on your smartphone. Your Alexa comes with skills built-in (like the ability to make a phone call, or check Wikipedia for information), and by adding additional skills, you can get Alexa to play quiz games, do an impression of Darth Vader, offer workout tips, plus much much more. In total, there are more than 100,000 skills available for Alexa worldwide, so chances are, if you can think of it, there's a skill for it.

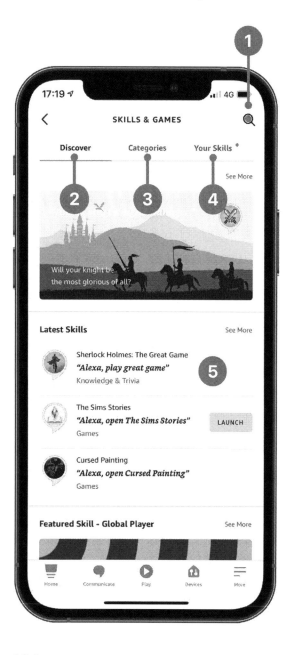

Explore skills for Alexa on your smartphone

To explore skills and games from your smartphone, open the Alexa app then tap **More > Skills & Games**.

1 If you have a skill in mind, try searching for it by tapping this button.

2 The Discover panel (seen here) let's you explore a range of curated skills.

3 Jump to a specific skills, such as Business & Finance or Games & Trivia.

4 Manage the skills you have already installed by tapping this option.

5 If you want to find out more about a skill, tap on it to see user reviews and enable it on your Echo device.

Explore skills for Alexa on your computer

While the smartphone app is a great way to explore skills and games, by using the larger screen of a laptop or desktop computer, you can see more skills at once, quickly jump between categories, and even enable skills on the Echo device linked to your account.

To find skills and games, go to Amazon website for your country or location (for example, in America, it's *www.amazon.com*, in Canada, it's *www.amazon.ca*, and in the UK, it's *www.amazon.co.uk*). Next, click the **All Departments** drop-down, choose **Alexa Skills**, then click the **search** button. Here's what you'll see next:

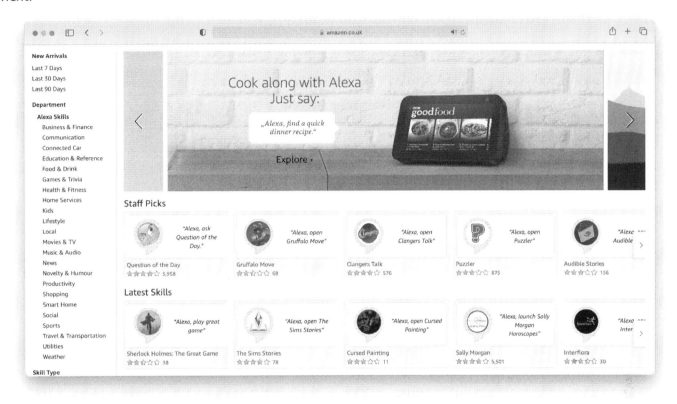

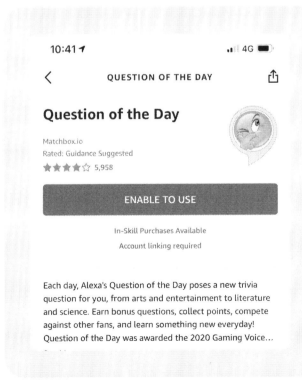

Enable a skill

If you've found a skill that looks interesting, feel free to enable it on your Echo. All skills are free, and if you decide that it's not worth your time, then you can also disable it using the Alexa app.

1. Open the Alexa app, tap the **More** button, choose **Skills & Games**, then find a skill that you would like to enable.

2. Tap **ENABLE TO USE**.

3. If the app requires information or permissions, then you'll see a panel appear. Set the permission switch to on, then tap **SAVE PERMISSIONS**.

4. The skill will then be enabled on your Echo.

Launch a skill

Once you've found and enabled a skill, you can activate it by saying:

"Alexa, open [skill]"   "Alexa, play [skill]"

"Alexa, launch [skill]"   "Alexa, start [skill]"

Make sure to replace [skill] with the name of the skill you have enabled.

To give you an example, if you wanted to play the Pointless Quiz Show on your Echo, you would first enable the skill called "Pointless", then you would say:

"Alexa, play Pointless"

Interact with a skill

Many skills have their own custom commands for performing actions. Perhaps a utility skill lets you unlock a door, or an audiobook skill lets you hear titles in your Audible library. To launch a skill and then interact with it, you would say:

"Alexa, ask [skill] to [task]"   "Alexa, open [skill] and [task]

To give an example, let's say you've enabled a skill that lets you use Alex's light ring to cast a glow over your bedroom at night (you can do this with the skill "Night Light"). If you wanted to turn on the light ring for the next 15 minutes, you would say:

"Alexa, open Night Light for 15 minutes"

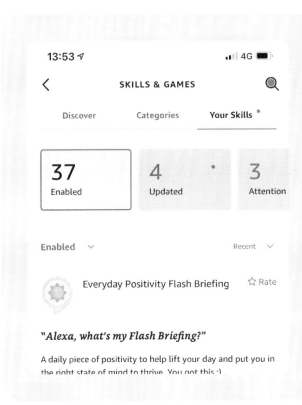

View your skills

Over time you'll likely accumulate a large number of Alexa skills. That's okay, as you can have as many as you'd like, but if you'd like to manage your skills, then here's how:

1 Open the Alexa app, tap the **More** button, choose **Skills & Games**.

2 Tap **Your Skills**.

3 Tap the **Recent** drop-down to sort skills alphabetically.

4 Tap the **Enabled** drop-down to see which skills are enabled, recently updated, or need your attention. If a skill needs your attention, then it likely requires you to at link an account with a third-party service.

Remove a skill

If you no longer need a skill, or if it has become unhelpful, then you can easily remove it by using the Amazon Alexa app.

1 Open the Alexa app, tap the **More** button, choose **Skills & Games**.

2 Tap **Your Skills**.

3 Tap on the skill that you would like to remove.

4 Tap **Disable Skill**.

5 The app will ask you to confirm and let you know that any skill-related information will also be deleted. Tap **DISABLE** if you're sure, and the skill will be removed from your Echo.

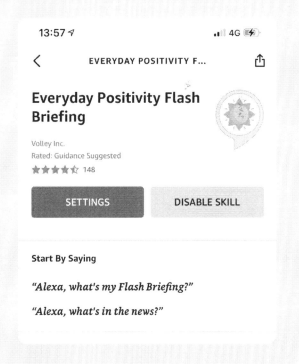

21 skills and games to try

Here are a few highlighted skills available for Alexa...

Whether you're looking for some daily humour, a mind-bending game, or some peace and quiet, here are 21 skills and games that you can enable on your Echo device...

7-Minute Workout

A scientifically proven set of exercises designed to increase metabolism, improve energy, lower stress, and best of all, remove fat! To begin, say, *"Alexa, start 7 Minute Workout"*.

Apple Music

Stream over 75 million songs ad-free from Apple Music, listen to your own playlists, and tune in to exclusive artist-hosted radio stations. Say, *"Alexa, play [artist] on Apple Music"*.

Knight Manager

A real-time construction game, where your job is to turn a small beach into a hip beach oasis. To stay playing, say, *"Alexa, open beach tycoon"*.

Big Sky®

Get a hyper-local for hour-by-hour forecasts tied to your actual street address, and locations around the world. To start, say, *"Alexa, open Big Sky"*.

Chewbacca Chat

Have a back and forth conversation with the the iconic wookiee Fuzz Ball. Chewie is a great listener and perfect to show off to your friends! Say, *"Alexa, open chewbacca chat"* to start.

Common Knowledge

Hosted by Joey Fatone, Common Knowledge is a game that asks those practical, everyday questions everyone should know.... but do you? To start, say, *"Alexa, play Common Knowledge"*.

Disney Stories

Listen to beloved Disney and Pixar stories, with magical read-aloud narration, music, and sound effects. Say, *"Alexa, ask Disney Stories for a Lion King story."*

ESPN

Get your sports radio fix with the ESPN skill, which includes ESPN radio and hourly news updates. Say, *"Alexa, play ESPN Radio"*.

Food Network Kitchen

Get cooking with your favourite Food Network stars, award-winning chefs and cookbook authors — all from your Echo Show! Say, *"Alexa, open Food Network Kitchen"*.

Headspace: Guided Meditation

Build a daily meditation practice, create the conditions for a better night's sleep, or go on guided walks and runs. You can say, *"Alexa, open Headspace"* to get started.

Inspire Me

Begin you day with some inspirational words from noted authors and famous figures. To get started, say *"Alexa, inspire me."*

Jeff Stelling's Sports Quiz

Test your ultimate sporting knowledge in this fun and competitive trivia game hosted by English sports journalist and TV presenter Jeff Stelling. Say, *"Alexa open Jeff Stelling's Sports Quiz".*

Knight Manager

An audio-based RPG game, where you make a glorious hero out of a weak amateur knight. Say, *"Alexa, start Knight Manager"* to start playing.

Quiz of the Day

Alexa's Quiz of the Day poses new fun & addictive trivia questions daily to give your brain some mental exercise! Say, *"Alexa, open Quiz of the Day."*

Ring

Use the Ring skill to manage all your Ring devices, such as smart cameras and door bells. Say, *"Alexa, show the front door"* to get started.

Sleep Sounds by Sleep Jar®

Play calming sound to help you fall asleep faster, sleep better, relax, meditate, or drown out distracting noises. To begin, say, *"Alexa, open Sleep Sounds".*

Spotify

Use Spotify to listen to music and podcasts, playlists, and even radio stations based on your music listening history. Say, *"Alexa, play [artist] on Spotify"* to start.

This Day In History

Check in with Alexa to find out about the historical events that happened on this day and every other day of the year. Say, *"Alexa, launch This Day in History".*

Trivia Battle

Trivia Battle is a daily trivia game where players from the various US states battle to get their state to the top of the smartness leaderboard. Say, *"Alexa, Open Trivia Battle".*

True or False

A fun game to test your knowledge about the world by answering either "true" or "false". The rules are simple, but the questions aren't. To begin, say, *"Alexa, play true or false".*

Xbox

Interact with your Xbox Series X|S or Xbox One using just your voice. Turn it on and off, launch games and apps, and play and pause videos. To get started, say, *"Alexa, tell Xbox to turn on."*

Create your own skill

Tell Alexa to say whatever you want...

As we discovered on the previous two pages, there are more than 100,000 additional skills available for Alexa, but did you know that you can also create your own? Well, technically, you're not creating skills from scratch; instead, you're able to customise more than 50 blueprints that Amazon has supplied. These blueprints cover everything from writing your own answers to questions, to creating your very own Spelling Bee, and each blueprint walks you through the steps of creating a skill. It's usually a case of writing *both* the questions and answers to a topic.

There's just one limitation to building your own skill: you can only use them with Echo devices signed in to your Amazon account. This means you can't share them on Amazon's Alexa Skills store or with friends and family.

Create a skill on your smartphone or tablet

The easiest way to create a skill is to use the Amazon Alexa app on your phone or tablet. To get started, open the app, tap **More** in the bottom corner, then choose **Skills & Games**.

1 Tap **Your Skills**, then swipe the boxes you see at the top of the screen towards the left, until a box appears called **Blueprint**.

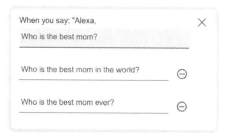

2 Tap **CREATE MORE SKILLS**. On the following screen, you can browse all the blueprints available for your Echo devices.

3 For this example, let's create a set of custom questions and answers. To do this, tap on **Custom Q&A**.

4 You'll then see a preview of the blueprint. To start building your own, tap **MAKE YOUR OWN** at the bottom of the screen.

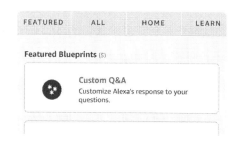

5 Look for the text fields that are prepopulated with questions and answers. Tap on them to add your own Q&As.

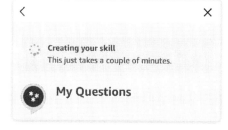

6 Tap **NEXT: CREATE SKILL**. After a minute or two, your skill will be ready, and you can invoke it by saying "*Alexa, open my questions*".

Create a skill on your computer

You might find it easier to create skills on your computer, where a larger screen gives you more space to breathe, and a physical keyboard makes it's easier to type. To get started on your computer, open a web browser, then go to *blueprints.amazon.com*. If the website suggests you visit the domain of your country (for example, *blueprints.amazon.ca,* then click on the recommendation).

One other note: make sure you're logged into your Amazon account on the desktop computer. If you see a "Sign In" button in the top-right corner, then click on it and log in before returning to *blueprints. amazon.com*. Next, let's create a custom Q&A....

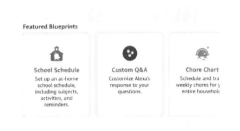

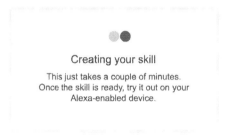

1 In the **Featured Blueprints** area near the top of the page, click **Custom Q&A**. Read the overview page to get an idea of how a custom Q&A works, then click **MAKE YOUR OWN**.

2 Look for the text fields that are prepopulated with questions and answers. Click on them to add your own Q&As.

3 Click **NEXT: CREATE SKILL**. After a minute or two, your skill will be ready, and you can invoke it by saying "*Alexa, open my questions*".

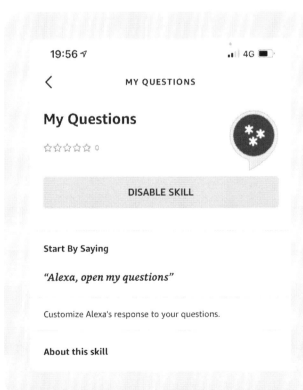

Delete a skill

If you'd like to disable a skill that you've made, then grab your smartphone or tablet and open the Amazon Alexa app. Then:

1 Tap the **More** button, then choose **Skills & Games**.

2 Tap **Your Skills**.

3 Swipe the boxes at the top of the screen towards the left until **Blueprint** appears.

4 Tap on the skill that you would like to delete.

5 Tap **DISABLE SKILL**, then on the following panel, confirm your choice by tapping **DISABLE**.

Learn about routines

Tell Alexa to do multiple things at once...

When you ask Alexa to do something, it's nearly always a one-off command, followed by a one-off response. Take checking the weather, for example. You might say, "Alexa, what's the weather like?" and Alexa will let you know. You might ask Alexa to start a phone call, set a timer, give you directions... it's usually a one-command/one-action routine.

This doesn't have to be the way because thanks to routines, you can give Alexa a single command, and it will respond with a chain of actions in quick succession. To give you an example, at the start of the day, you might want to turn Alexa to turn on all the lights, give you a weather report, tell you the latest news headlines, then inform you of any calendar events ahead.

Without a routine, you would have to command Alexa to perform each action, but *with* a routine, you would only need to say something like, "*Alexa, good morning*", and Alexa would perform each of those steps above.

What actions you can include in a routine

When creating a routine for Alexa, there are more than 15 actions you can include. You might even see more if you have smart devices and third-party apps set up for Alexa). Here's a round-up of each action:

- **Alexa says:** Alexa will say a preset phrase (such as "good morning"), a custom phrase (like "hey good looking"), sing a song, tell a joke, or tell a story.

- **Audible:** Alexa will read one of your books from Audible.

- **Calendar:** Alexa will let you know of any events for the day ahead, tomorrow, or the next event.

- **Calling:** Alexa will enable calling on your Echo devices for the day ahead.

- **Date and Time:** Alexa will tell you the date and time.

- **Device settings:** You can set the device volume, stop any audio, or enable Do Not Disturb mode.

- **E-Mail:** Alexa will ready your e-mail summary.

- **Fire TV:** Alexa will play content on any Fire TV devices you have.

- **Messaging:** Alexa will read any notificcations or send an announcement to your Echo devices.

- **Music & Podcasts:** Play a song, artist, or podcasts. You can also set a music playback duration.

- **News:** Alexa will play news from your Flash Briefing.

- **Smart Home:** Control smart devices or groups of devices.

- **Sounds:** Alexa will play a sound effect (such as a cow mooing).

- **Traffic:** Get a live traffic report for your area.

- **Wait:** Add a pause to the action routine.

- **Weather:** Alexa will report the weather for your area.

Create a routine

Start your day with a routine from Alexa...

You can make routines as simple or complex as you like, and it's possible to have multiple routines to cater for every aspect of your life. To get started, let's create a routine where Alexa gives us the morning news, followed by the weather...

1. Go to routines

Open the Alexa app, tap **More** in the bottom corner, then tap **Routines**. On the following screen, tap the **plus** button in the top corner.

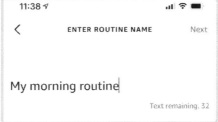

2. Give your routine a name

Tap on **Enter routine name**, then enter a name using the keyboard. Tap **Next** to continue.

3. Set a routine trigger

Tap **When this happens**. You can now choose how to trigger a routine. For this example, tap **Voice**, then use the keyboard to type "*good morning*". Tap **Next** when you're finished.

4. Choose an action

Tap **Add Action**, then make a choice of action type, for example, News. Tap **Next** once you've made a choice.

5. Add additional actions

To add additional actions, tap the **Add action** button and make a choice. For this example, tap **Weather**, then **Next**.

6. Save your routine

When you've added all your actions, tap **Save** in the top corner.

Run your routine

When you're ready to run the routine that we have created above, all you need to do is say:

"Alexa, good morning"

Chapter 09

Create a smart home

You've probably heard of smart devices and smart homes, and you might be wondering what exactly a "smart" device is? There are many definitions, depending on who you ask, but in short, a smart device lets you control it over the internet.

Let's explore an example, in this case, a "smart light". It might take the form of a light bulb that connects to the web, or it could be a traditional old fashioned lamp that is plugged into a smart plug socket. Either way, because this is a smart light, you can turn it on or off by saying, "Alexa, turn off smart light". This isn't the only benefit of a smart light; you can also set up timers using Alexa, then automatically turn your home lights off at sunrise and back on at sunset. You can also save yourself from having to physically get up and press the light switch on the other side of the room.

Hopefully, you're getting the idea of how smart devices work and how they can transform your life. Other smart devices include door locks, cameras, baby monitors, thermostats... the list is endless. In this chapter, we'll take a look at how you can set up a smart home, connect devices to Alexa, and then enrich your life by saving time and effort.

In this chapter:

Understand the basics of smart devices

Discover what a smart device is...

Smart devices are slowly making their way into homes, much to the benefit of those who reside within them. While there's always the potential for hackers to spy on a camera, or flick lights on and off, thankfully, it almost never happens (can you recall the last time a news story broke about smart devices being hacked?) This is in part due to modern encryption methods -- which scrambles your information as it travels over the internet before descrambling it at the other end -- and the use of better security practices at both Amazon and the manufacturers who make smart devices.

As we covered on the previous page, smart devices use the internet to transmit data and their controls, and when you break it down, there are four benefits to using them:

Automation

Smart devices can take information about the world around them and do clever things. Take thermostats, for example. A "dumb" thermostat can tell the temperature, and that's about it. A smart thermostat can schedule heating, generate reports of energy usage, and even monitor movement within the home to heat those areas where people are present.

Time saving

Smart devices can save you from having to perform daily chores or even get up out of your seat. Take garage door openers, for example. A smart garage opener can connect to your phone and car, then automatically open the garage as you drive up to it, which means no more getting out of the car to haul up a heavy door, just to put the car away.

Lots of information

A typical door lock won't give you any information. It's literally a lock, with no bells or whistles. With a smart lock, you can learn who exactly has been going in and out and at what times.

Additional security

You've just learned that smart locks can offer information on who is entering your home and when, but did you also know that smart locks (as well as many other smart devices) can offer additional security too? The August Smart Lock, for example, and can create virtual keys for guests and an auto-lock and unlock function. Shop around, and you'll also find smart locks that feature fingerprint sensors or support for Key by Amazon, which lets delivery drivers drop off parcels *within* your home.

Setting up a smart device

It's not exactly "plug and go"...

The biggest barrier to setting up a smart home is where to start. You might have a lot of questions, like how do I set up a smart device? And how do I control it? Unfortunately, there's no simple answer as each smart device has its own set up process, so it's difficult to go into specific. In general, however, the flow goes like this...

Step 1 | **Buy a smart device**
Take your time shopping around, as there are often a massive range of smart devices for each category. Look for devices with a high user rating, and make sure whatever you buy works with Alexa. You'll know because it will say "Works with Alexa" in the description or item name.

Step 2 | **Install the smartphone app**
Once your smart device arrives, install the manufacturers app on your smartphone or tablet. The box or manual will let you know which app to look for.

Step 3 | **Set up your smart device**
Plug in your smart device, wait for it to turn on, then use the manufacturers app to set it up. Usually this involves creating an account with the manufacturer, registering the device, then connecting it to your home's Wi-Fi connection.

Step 4 | **Use Alexa to find the device**
With your smart device up and running, the next step is to connect it to Alexa. Flip over the page for more details on this process.

Step 5 | **Start using your smart device**
Once Alexa is connected, you can start controlling the smart device with either voice commands or by using the Alexa app. Once you're comfortable using the smart device, then you might also set up schedules for timers, profiles for locks, and scenes for rooms with multiple devices. We'll cover all of this over the next few pages.

Add smart devices to Alexa

Find your new smart device, and select a category...

As we explored on the previous page, there are many types of smart devices, from many manufacturers, that all have a slightly different set-up process. In general, you need to install the device's associated app, plug in the device, then connect it to your home Wi-Fi network. With those steps completed, it's time to tell Alexa about the new device, then take your first steps into the world of smart lights, plugs, cameras, locks, and more...

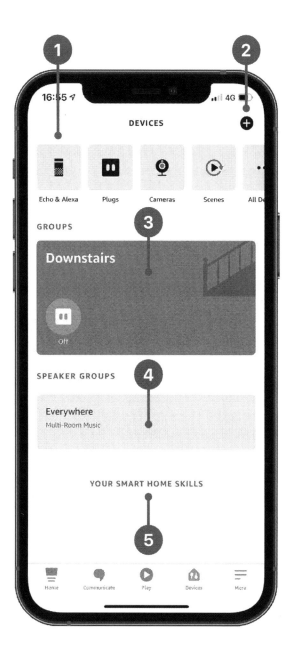

An overview of the Devices panel in the Alexa app

Before we start adding devices and groups, here's a quick overview of the Devices area of the Alexa app. To find it, simply open the Alexa app, then tap **Devices**.

1 Explore your Echo devices using these shortcuts at the top of the screen.

2 Tap the **plus** button to add a new device or group of devices (see across page for more).

3 This panel represents a group of devices. In this example, the group comprises smart plugs located on the downstairs floor of a house.

4 This grey panel represents a group of speakers. Turn over the page to learn more about adding groups of speakers.

5 Tap this link to explore Alexa skills that are specific to your smart devices. For example, if you have smart plugs in your home, then you'll see Alexa skills that enable you to power those plugs on and off.

Add a smart device

After powering up your smart device and then setting it up using the manufacturer's app, it's time to add the device to Alexa. Rather cleverly, many smart devices will automatically connect to Alexa once you open the Amazon Alexa app, but if this isn't the case and you'd like to manually add the device, follow these instructions:

1 Open the Alexa app, then tap **Devices**.

2 Tap the **plus** button in the top corner.

3 Choose **Add Device**, then select the type of smart device you're adding.

4 After choosing a device type, look for the brand name, then tap on it.

5 If the device doesn't automatically connect, tap the **DISCOVER DEVICES** button and wait for the Alexa app to find your new device. Tap **Done** once it is found.

16:19

< SETUP ?

Connect your eFamilyCloud device to Alexa

1. Download the eFamilyCloud app.
2. Set up your eFamilyCloud device following the eFamilyCloud app instructions
3. Return to the Alexa app.
4. Press Discover Devices.

16:28 ... 4G

< CREATE GROUPS ?

Create rooms, device groups and large areas

Create a room or device group
Make it easier to turn on lights, play music or control devices in a room

Combine rooms or groups
Control larger areas of your home or play music in multiple rooms

Create a group of smart devices

If you have multiple smart devices within your home, then it's a good idea to group them by room, area, or floor. By doing this you can do things like turn on all the lights in a room, or play music throughout an entire area of your home.

1 To create a group, open the Alexa app, tap **Devices**, then tap the **plus** button.

2 Choose **Add Group.**

3 Tap **Create a room or device group** if you're starting off for the first time, then tap **NEXT**.

4 Select a name for the group, or scroll to the bottom of the screen to create a custom name, then tap **NEXT**.

5 Select the smart devices you would like to add to the group, then tap **NEXT**.

6 If you have multiple Echo's in your home, then you can also add these to your group. If so, select them, then tap **NEXT**.

7 Your group is now ready to use.

Add a group of speakers

Let's say you have multiple Echo devices in your home. By grouping these speakers together -- for example, all the speakers downstairs -- you can then say to Alexa, "*Alexa, play music on the [name] group*", and hear sweet music throughout each room of that area. To create a group of speakers:

1 Open the Alexa app, then tap **Devices**.

2 Tap the **plus** button in the top corner.

3 Choose **Combine speakers**, then choose **Multi-room music**.

4 On the following screen, tap on each Eacho that you would like to group together, then tap Next.

5 Choose a name for the group. To create a name of your own, scroll to the bottom of the screen and tap on **Customised Name**.

6 Tap **Save** and the group of speakers will appear on the Devices panel within the Alexa app. You can now play music via this group by saying, "*Alexa, play music on the [name] group*".

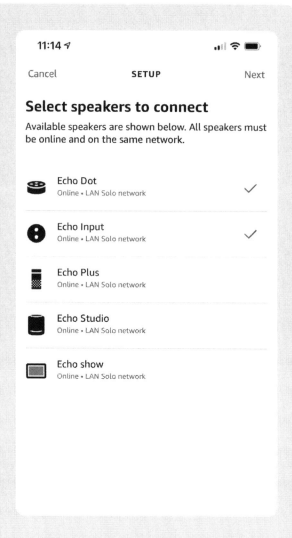

Rename a smart device

If, like me, you have a lot of similar smart devices throughout your home, then it's a good idea to give them unique names. You might name a device based on its location or its function; whatever is easy to remember. Here's how to rename a smart device using the Alexa app:

1 Open the Alexa app, then tap **Devices**.

2 Use the shortcuts at the top of the screen to select the category of device.

3 From the category area, tap on the device you would like to rename, then tap the **settings** button in the top corner.

4 Next, tap **Edit Name**, then enter a new name using the keyboard. When you're finished, tap the **back arrow** in the top-left corner.

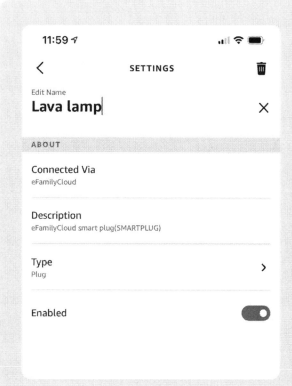

Change the device type

Alexa can tell the difference between a plug, a lock, a camera, and many more device types. Sometimes, however, it can be helpful to change the device type to enable extra features. Say, for example, you have a lamp plugged into a smart plug. By changing the device from a plug to a light, you can then control the device by saying, "Alexa, turn on the light". To change types:

1 Open the Alexa app, then tap **Devices**, then use the shortcuts at the top of the screen to select the category of device.

2 From the category area, tap on the device you would like to change, then tap the **settings** button in the top corner.

3 Tap on **Type**, then select a new type of device by using the buttons (see image to the right).

4 Tap **DONE** to save your changes. Alexa will now treat the device as the type you've selected.

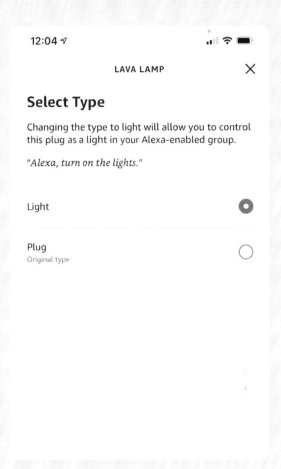

Delete a smart device or group of devices

If you need to remove a smart device or even an entire group of devices, then here's what to do:

1 To create a group, open the Alexa app, then tap **Devices**.

2 To remove a smart device, select the category of device at the top of the screen.

3 From the category area, tap on the device you would like to remove, then tap the **settings** button in the top corner.

4 Next, tap the **trash** button in the top corner, then confirm by tapping **Delete**.

5 To remove a group, tap **Devices**, select the group, then tap **UNPAIR** at the bottom of the screen.

Control smart devices

Learn what to say to your family of smart devices...

With your home now set up with a collection of smart devices and Echo's, it's time to start taking advantage of it by using voice commands to toggle switches on, adjust ambient lights, and control the temperature in your home. To get you started, here are some commands you can use with Alexa...

Control smart plugs

Smart plugs are surprisingly helpful. Not only do they turn things on and off, but you can also use the manufacturer's app to schedule the plugs to power on and off at specific times.

"Alexa, turn [device name] on"   "Alexa, turn [device name] off"

Remember to replace [device name] with the name of your smart device.

Control smart cameras

Protecting your home with smart cameras is a great way to catch thieves in the act, but you can also monitor children or pets when you're in a different room or away from home. There are usually three types of smart camera: the outdoor type that acts as a surveillance camera, the indoor type that can track movement and even identify family members, and the doorbell type that can show you who's at the door.

Whichever type of camera you own, it's a good idea to have an Echo device with a screen (such as an Echo Show), as this can show the camera's video feed by using the following command:

"Alexa, show [device name]"

Make sure to replace [device name] with the name of your camera. When you've finished watching the camera, say:

"Alexa, hide [device name]"

Control smart lights

Regular light switches don't do anything particularly exciting. They turn on. They turn off. They also have one brightness setting, unless you have a dimmer control on the wall. Smart lights, however, are so much more exciting. Not only can you flick them on and off, but you can often control their brightness and colour and even automate them to come on at sunset, then turn off at a specific time (you'll need to use the manufacturer's app for that). For the basic controls, here's what you can say to Alexa:

"Alexa, turn [device name] on"   "Alexa, turn [device name] off"

Remember to replace [device name] with the name of your smart light. For smart lights that can adjust their brightness, try saying:

"Alexa, brighten [device name]"   "Alexa, dim [device name]"

And for smart lights that can change colour, say:

"Alexa, set [device name] to [colour]"

Control smart thermostats

If you've installed a smart thermostat and connected it to Alexa, then here are some commands to try:

"Alexa, set [device name] to cool"   "Alexa, what is [device name] set to?"

"Alexa, set [device name] to heat"   "Alexa, set [device name] to [number] degrees"

"Alexa, set [device name] to auto"

"Alexa, turn [device name] off"   "Alexa, increase [device name] by [number] degrees"

"Alexa, what is [device name]'s temperature?"   "Alexa, decrease [device name] by [number] degrees"

Remember to replace [device name] with the name of your smart thermostat.

Control smart speakers

The Echo isn't the only smart speaker that works with Alexa. You'll also find smart speakers from Bose, Sonos, Ultimate Ears, Denon, and Audio Pro. Here are some of the commands you can use with not only the Echo but other Alexa-compatible smart speakers:

"Alexa, play [artist/album/song] on [device name]"

"Alexa, pause"

"Alexa, play"

"Alexa, next track"

"Alexa, set the volume to [number]"

"Alexa, set the bass to [number]"

Control groups of speakers

If you have grouped multiple sets of speakers around your home (for example, all the speakers downstairs), then you can can play music across all of them by saying:

"Alexa, play music on the downstairs group"

Make sure to replace "*downstairs*" with the name of your group. Once music is playing, you can control it using these commands:

"Alexa, next on [group name]"

"Alexa, previous on [group name]"

"Alexa, restart song on [group name]"

"Alexa, volume [number] on [group name]"

"Alexa, play [artist/album/track] on [group name]"

"Alexa, play [artist] station" on [group name]"

"Alexa, play something new on [group name]"

Control smart locks

With a smart lock in your home, you can lock and unlock doors remotely, set a PIN number to protect your home, and even set up fingerprint access. There are quite a few specific commands available for these devices, but here are the commost commonly used:

"Alexa, lock [device name]"   "Alexa, unlock [device name]"

If you're not sure if you've locked the house and want to check on the status of a lock, say:

"Alexa, is the (device name) locked / unlocked?"

Other smart device commands

There are a huge amount of smart devices available for Alexa, all with their own smartphone apps and many with custom commands that only work with specific devices. Here are a few examples:

- If you have a smart oven from General Electric, you can preheat the oven by saying, "*Alexa, tell Geneva to preheat my oven to 400 degrees*".

- With a smart washing machine from General Electric, you can check on the status of your laundry by saying, "*Alexa, ask Geneva if my laundry is dry*".

- If you have a smart garage door opener from Garageio, you can open and close it by saying, "*Alexa, ask Garageio to close my garage*".

- With a Logitech Harmony Hub, you can control your smart TV by saying, "*Alexa, turn on the TV*", or "*Alexa, turn on Netflix*".

Chapter 10

Discover Alexa's funny side

So you're starting to get familiar with Alexa. You've set up your Echo, explored the basics, made a phone call, even created a skill. What next? Well, there's an entire world of additional things you can ask Alexa. You can ask Alexa to tell a joke, sing a song, and even entertain your pet.

In this chapter:

Ask Alexa to tell a joke

Alexa might think in code, but it still has a funny sense of humour...

Alexa is usually straight-talking. It gets right to the point, following your commands and offering information on nearly anything you can think of, but it also has a funny side. If you want to get to know Alexa a little bit better, then ask it to tell you a joke. You'll soon discover that it has a rather corny sense of humour...

"Alexa, tell me a joke"

"Alexa, make me laugh"

"Alexa, tell me a dad joke"

"Alexa, tell me a dirty joke"

"Alexa, tell me a 'yo mama' joke"

"Alexa, tell me a knock-knock joke"

"Alexa, tell me a blooper"

"Alexa, tell me a tounge twister"

Ask for a specific category of jokes

Alexa knows a lot about culture, people, and history, so you can ask it to tell a joke about a specific category, and it will quickly come up with something. Here's how it works:

"Alexa, tell me a [topic] joke"

Replace [topic] with something you can think of. Here are some examples:

"Alexa, tell me a Star Wars joke"

"Alexa, tell me an aliens joke"

"Alexa, tell me a Christmas joke"

"Alexa, tell me a football joke"

"Alexa, tell me a maths joke"

"Alexa, tell me a history joke"

"Alexa, tell me a cat joke"

"Alexa, tell me a technology joke"

Ask Alexa to sing

Alexa is surprisingly good at holding a tune...

While Alexa is great at talking to you in a clear and concise manner, did you know that it can also serenade you with a wide range of songs? Whether it's your birthday, it's Christmas, or you simply want to entertain your dog, here are some commands you can use to hear Alexa sing a song...

"Alexa, sing a song"	"Alexa, sing a lullaby"
"Alexa, sing a Christmas carol"	"Alexa, rap for me!"
"Alexa, sing 'Happy Birthday'"	"Alexa, wash my hands"
"Alexa, sing a love song"	"Alexa, sing the national anthem"
"Alexa, sing the ABCs"	"Alexa, sing: Happy in the cloud!"
"Alexa, sing Auld Lang Syne"	"Alexa, yodel for me"
"Alexa, sing in auto-tune"	"Alexa, sing a cowboy/girl song"

Listen to an Alexa song

If Alexa wasn't a personal assistant, then it might have taken up a career as a songwriter because she has secretly written 17 catchy songs that you can listen to by using the following command:

"Alexa, sing [songname]"

Replace [songname] with one of the following:

- The Pirate Song
- In the Moonlight Tonight
- Woohoo Technology
- The Ballad of the Broken S'more
- Sand Beneath Your Toes / Summer Song
- Love Song
- It's raining in the cloud
- Take Me Out to the Ball Game
- Will You Marry Me
- Alexa's Theme Song
- The No Body Blues
- Things that go Bump in the Night
- Colonel Doggy
- Model of a Digital Intelligence
- The Thank You Song
- Paper Airplanes
- The Space Song

Entertain the kids (or pet)

These commands will keep the kids happy, for a while...

Alexa has some tricks up its sleeve for keeping the children happy. It can play tell a story, play a short word game, or even make animal sound effects.

"Alexa, entertain me?"

"Alexa, meow"

"Alexa, bark"

"Alexa, ask Pikachu to talk"

"Alexa, can we play an animal game?"

"Alexa, tell me a story?"

"Alexa, begin my Jedi lessons"

"Alexa, do you like green eggs and ham?"

"Alexa, read me a Kindle book" (It will read you the last book you downloaded on Amazon)

"Alexa, open Animal Workout"

" Alexa, open Sesame Street"

"Alexa, start science quiz"

"Alexa, where's Santa?"

"Alexa, start No Way That's True"

" Alexa, open Jurassic World"

"Alexa, ask for a fart"

Play animal sounds

If you have a cat or dog then in the house, then you can really drive them wild by playing animal sounds through your Echo. To start, say:

"Alexa, moo like a cow"

After the cow has mooed, you can ask for Alexa to play one of dozens of animal sound effects, including:

- Baboon
- Bear
- Blackbird
- Bobcat
- Cat
- Chicken
- Coyote
- Dog
- Dolphin
- Hippopotamus
- Lemur
- Lion
- Owl
- Parrot
- Pig
- Spider
- Magpie
- Monkey
- Sheep
- Spider monkey
- Squirrel
- Rat
- Rooster

Try a wordplay game

Give you brain a challenge...

If you're feeling like taxing your brain with a clever wordplay or tongue-twister, then here are some things to ask Alexa:

"Alexa, tell me a riddle"

"Alexa, tell me a puzzle"

"Alexa, tell me a tongue-twister"

"Alexa, tell me a haiku"

"Alexa, tell me a pun"

"Alexa, tell me a rhyme"

"Alexa, tell me an oxymoron"

"Alexa, tell me a limerick"

"Alexa, tell me a palindrome"

"Alexa, tell me some Pig Latin"

Ask Alexa for the longest word...

If you want to really challenge yourself with a tongue-twister, then try asking Alexa for the longest word by saying:

"Alexa, tell me the longest word"

In case you're wondering, it's pneumonoultramicroscopicsilicovolcanoconiosis.

Play Philosoraptor

To challenge your perception of the world, say to Alexa:

"Alexa, open Philosoraptor"

Alexa will then give you some food for though, such as " If actions are stronger than words, then why is the pen mightier than the sword?", and, "If camera lenses are round, why do pictures come out rectangular?"

Ask Alexa to be silly

If you need a chuckle, just ask Alexa something silly...

Artificial intelligence doesn't have to be serious or get straight to the point. Alexa proves this by providing a wealth of silly answers, games, and sound effects.

Silly questions to ask Alexa

Give Alexa something fun to do by asking one of these commands:

"Alexa, can you cough?"

"Alexa, can you bark?"

"Alexa, can you burp?"

"Alexa, can you cry like a baby?"

"Alexa, make me a sandwich"

"Alexa, drumroll"

"Alexa, self-destruct"

"Alexa, pretend to be a superhero"

"Alexa, do you know Siri?"

"Alexa, Mac or PC?"

"Alexa, are you a robot?"

"Alexa, what are the three laws of robotics?"

"Alexa, are we in the Matrix?"

"Alexa, flush the toilet"

"Alexa, surely you can't be serious?"

"Alexa, where is Chuck Norris?"

"Alexa, roll a die"

"Alexa, what's the meaning of life?"

"Alexa, how was your day?"

"Alexa, what should I wear today?"

"Alexa, what are you thinking about?"

"Alexa, do you believe in love at first sight?"

"Alexa, are you pretty?"

"Alexa, how old are you?"

"Alexa, who is your best friend?"

"Alexa, do you have a boyfriend/girlfriend?"

"Alexa, what's your favorite color?"

"Alexa, where do you live?"

"Alexa, who is the voice of Alexa?"

"Alexa, how tall are you?"

"Alexa, what do you want to be when you grow up?"

Easter eggs to try

Not literal eggs, but something more funny...

Before you ask, we're not talking about actual Easter eggs here (although if you're feeling peckish, then you can order Easter eggs from Amazon by saying, *"Alexa, order Easter eggs"*). Instead, we're talking about the digital type of Easter egg, which is something virtual that's hidden away in the code of a program or system.

There are dozens, maybe even hundreds of Easter eggs hidden away in Alexa's code. We'll explore a few of them over the next couple of pages, but if you'd like to recieve a random one, then say:

"Alexa, tell me an Easter egg"

Music Easter eggs

If you're looking for a music-themed Easter egg, try saying:

"Alexa, who let the dogs out?"

"Alexa, do you really want to hurt me?"

"Alexa, I shot a man in Reno"

"Alexa, what is the loneliest number?"

"Alexa, how many roads must a man walk down?"

"Alexa, how much is that doggie in the window?"

"Alexa, who is the walrus?"

"Alexa, why do birds suddenly appear?"

"Alexa, never gonna give you up"

"Alexa, twinkle twinkle little star"

"Alexa, my milkshake brings all the boys to the yard"

"Alexa, is this the real life?"

"Alexa, I like big butts"

"Alexa, what is war good for?"

"Alexa, have you ever seen the rain?"

"Alexa, hello, it's me"

Film & TV Easter eggs

"Alexa, may the force be with you"

"Alexa, that's no moon"

"Alexa, I shot a man in Reno"

"Alexa, do you feel lucky punk?"

"Alexa, your mother was a hamster!"

"Alexa, who you gonna call?"

"Alexa, are we in the Matrix?"

"Alexa, supercalifragilisticexpialodocious"

"Alexa, define rock paper scissors lizard spock"

"Alexa, I want to play global thermonuclear war"

"Alexa, do you want to build a snowman?"

"Alexa, why so serious?"

"Alexa, who is the mother of dragons?"

"Alexa, is Jon Snow dead?"

"Alexa, more cowbell"

"Alexa, this is a dead parrot"

"Alexa, who shot JR?"

Miscellaneous Easter eggs

"Alexa, why did the chicken cross the road?"

"Alexa, which comes first: the chicken or the egg?"

"Alexa, what is the meaning of life?"

"Alexa, where's Waldo?"

"Alexa, who's the boss?"

"Alexa, what is the sound of one hand clapping?"

"Alexa, one fish two fish"

"Alexa, this statement is false"

"Alexa, why is a raven like a writing desk?"

"Alexa, how many pickled peppers did Peter Piper pick?"

"Alexa, give me some money"

"Alexa, are you lying?"

"Alexa, will pigs fly?"

"Alexa, testing..."

"Alexa, do aliens exist? "

"Alexa, happy birthday!"

"Alexa, take me to your leader!"

"Alexa, is there life on Mars?"

"Alexa, what are the laws of robotics?"

"Alexa, tell me something interesting."

"Alexa, what should I wear today?"

"Alexa, flip a coin"

"Alexa, Cheers!"

Chapter 11

Privacy and security

H aving a personal assistant in your home is pretty fantastic, but when you think about it from a privacy perspective, there are some obvious concerns. First of all, you've installed a device that's constantly listening to everything you say. Sure, it only activates when a specific "wake word" is said, but Alexa still needs to listen to everything around it to ensure it hears the correct word. Second, if you have an Echo Spot or Show, then you've basically installed a webcam in your home. Other privacy concerns include sending personal information across the internet and the ability for anyone to make a purchase using your Echo device.

Before you panic, consider that Amazon's entire business is run over the internet. The company has successfully managed customers' personal details, shopping history, and communications for more than 25 years. It also powers nearly one-third of the internet. It does this by providing the servers and computing power that run many of the websites and cloud services used by businesses today.

Could your personal information ever leak outside of Amazon? It's not impossible, but it's very, very unlikely. That being said, this chapter will explain how you can ensure your personal details stay safe while using Alexa.

In this chapter:

Automatically delete your voice recordings

Delete recordings of your interactions with Alexa...

Whenever you interact with Alexa, a recording of your voice is sent to Amazon, processed, and then a response is sent back. By default, these recordings are stored indefinitely. This is to give Amazon the opportunity to learn how you interact with Alexa and to better understand your voice. Effectively, over time your experience with Alexa should improve, and the voice recognition should get better.

It's worth noting that only an extremely small fraction of voice recordings are manually reviewed. That being said, you might not feel comfortable having recordings of your voice, conversations, and sounds from your home being stored on the internet. Thankfully, Amazon provides an easy way to automatically delete these recordings after a set period of time.

Choose how long to save recordings

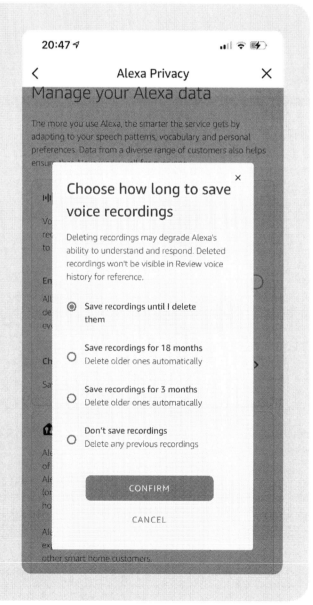

Start by opening the Amazon Alexa app on your smartphone or tablet, then:

1. Tap **More** in the bottom corner, then choose **Settings**.

2. Tap **Alexa Privacy**.

3. Tap **Manage Your Alexa Data**.

4. Read the following screen to get an understanding of how voice recordings are used. When you're ready to change how long they are saved, tap **Choose how long to save recordings**.

5. In the pop-up window, choose from one of the following options:

   • Until you want to delete them manually (indefinitely)

   • Delete recordings after 18 months.

   • Delete recordings after 3 months.

   • Don't save any recordings.

6. Once you've made a choice, tap **CONFIRM**.

Change Alexa's Wake Word

Say something other than "Alexa"...

Everytime you interact with Alexa, you stand near your Echo and say, "*Alexa...*" There's a good reason why this particular word was chosen: it has a hard consonant with the X, which helps for the word to be recognised with high precision. It's also reminiscent of the Great Library of Alexandria, one of the largest and most significant libraries of the ancient world.

If you're tired of saying "Alexa" all the time, or find that your Echo device is regularly picking up words that sound like Alexa, then there are a small handful of other Wake Words that you can use: Amazon, Computer, and Echo. To choose one of these...

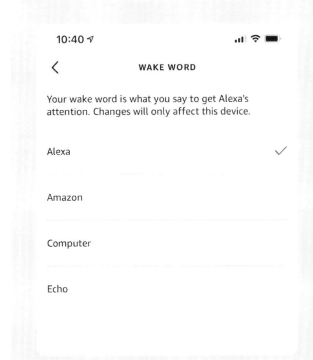

Choose a new Wake Word

To choose a Wake Word other than "Alexa":

1. Open the Amazon Alexa app on your smartphone or tablet, then tap **Devices**.

2. Tap on your Echo or Echo dot.

3. Scroll down, then tap **Wake Word**. On the following screen, you will see these options: Alexa, Amazon, Computer, and Echo.

4. Tap on your option of choice, tap **OK** if a pop-up window appears, then wait a few minutes for your Echo device to update itself. You can then activate Alexa using the new Wake Word.

If you're wondering which one to choose, consider this: in 2020, CNET tested each Wake Word to see which one was accidentally triggered the least amount of times. It turns out that "Computer" was triggered the least, followed by "Amazon", then "Echo", then "Alexa".

137

Manage your data

Review your voice history and smart device history...

Alexa is constantly recording a wealth of data covering how and when you interact with it. This is helpful in that the more you use Alexa, the smarter the services becomes by adapting to your speech patterns, vocabulary, and personal preferences. If you're worried about all of this data being stored on the internet and want to review your recent activity with Alexa, then grab your smartphone, open the Alexa app, and following these instructions:

Review your voice history

To view your recent interactions with Alexa, or delete your voice history, open the Amazon Alexa app on your smartphone or tablet, and then:

1 Tap **More** in the bottom corner, then choose **Settings**.

2 Tap **Alexa Privacy**.

3 Tap **Review Voice History**.

4 You'll see an overview of your interactions with Alexa for the current day. To view more history, or to choose a specific Echo device, tap the up arrow next to **Displaying**, then choose an option.

5 To delete your recent recordings, tap **Delete all recordings from last 7 days**, then tap **DELETE** in the pop-up window.

6 To listen to an individual recording, tap the **down arrow** next to the transcription, then tap the **play** button.

7 To delete a specific recording, tap the **down arrow** next to the transcription, then tap the **trash** button.

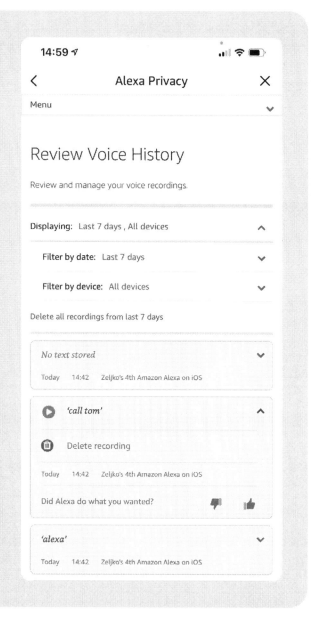

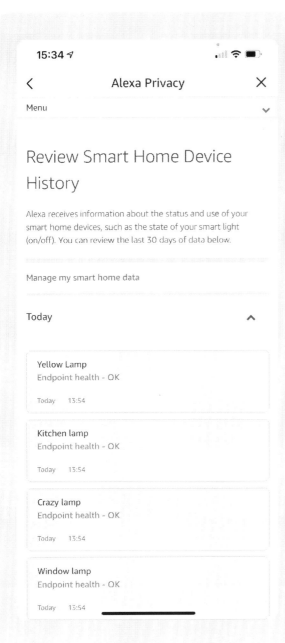

Review your smart device history

If you have any smart devices within your home, such as smart lights, locks, or cameras, then Alexa stores the recent statuses of these devices. If you would like to review or delete this history, then:

1 Open the Amazon Alexa app on your smartphone or tablet.

2 Tap **More** in the bottom corner, choose **Settings**, then tap **Alexa Privacy**.

3 Tap **Review Smart Home Device History**.

4 On the following screen, tap the down arrow next to a date, and you'll see information about the statuses of your smart devices.

5 To manage this histroy, tap **Manage my smart home data**, then scroll down until Smart home device history appears.

6 Tap **Choose how long to save history**, to save your device history indefinitely (default), for 18 months or three months.

7 Tap **One-off deletion of all history** to do just that - delete all of your smart device history.

8 Tap **Email complete history** to receive a CSV file with the status and usage information for all of your devices.

Tell Amazon to not review your recordings

It rarely happens, but sometimes recordings from Alexa are reviewed manually by a team within Amazon. This helps them to train Alexa to become more accurate. If you would like to tell Amazon not to review any of your interactions with Alexa, then:

1 Open the Amazon Alexa app on your smartphone or tablet.

2 Tap **More** in the bottom corner, choose **Settings**, then tap **Alexa Privacy**.

3 Tap **Manage your Alexa data**.

4 Scroll down until a panel appears called **Help improve Alexa**. Toggle the top switch off, and no recordings will ever be reviewed.

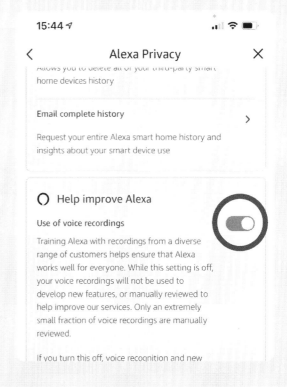

Disable communication and video features

Turn off messages, Drop In, and access to your contacts...

Some of Alexa's most unique features are based around communication, such as the ability to send messages, drop in on another Echo, and make audio or video calls. There are some inherent risks to these features, however, including:

• It's helpful to have access to your contacts list on Alexa, but eavesdroppers could potentially overhear personal details, or Alexa could accidentally send a message on your behalf.

• Enabling Drop In on your Echo means anyone in your contacts list could begin a voice or video call without you knowing.

• Messages sent using Alexa arrive as audio clips. There's a very remote possibility that a hacker could embed malicious code in audio form, then get access to your Echo or Amazon account.

If any of these issues concern you, then here's how to disable communication features on your Echo.

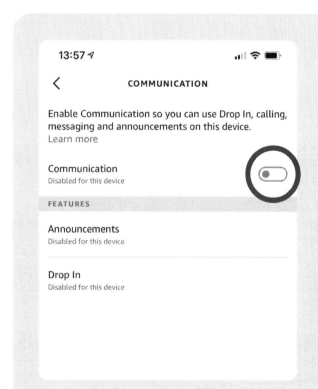

Turn all communications off in one go

If you don't plan to use any of Alexa's communication features, then you can quickly disable them all from the Alexa app. To do this:

1 Open the Amazon Alexa app on your smartphone or tablet, then tap **Devices**.

2 Tap on your Echo device.

3 Scroll down, then tap **Communication**.

4 Toggle the **Communication** switch off.

5 If you would like to disable either announcements or Drop In, tap their respective options from this screen, then toggle them off.

Disable access to your contacts

If you have turned off the communication features on your Echo, then you no longer need to give Alexa access to your contacts list. To disable it:

1. Open the Amazon Alexa app on your smartphone or tablet.

2. Tap **More** in the bottom corner, then choose **Settings**.

3. Scroll down, then tap **Communication**.

4. Tap **Manage Contacts**, then choose **Import Contacts**.

5. Toggle **Import Contacts** off, then confirm when the app asks you.

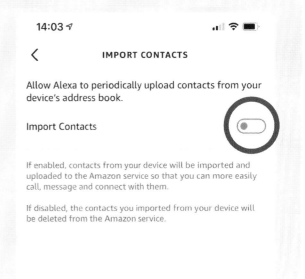

Turn off the microphone and camera

If you're feeling particularly untrustworthy of Alexa, then it's possible to quickly disable the microphone, and if you have an Echo Spot or Show, then the camera too.

Turn off the microphone on an Echo, Echo Dot, and Echo Studio

Push the microphone on/off button on the top of your Echo. When the microphone is disabled, the light ring will turn red to let you know. Your Echo will not respond until you reactivate the microphone by pushing the mic on/off button again.

Turn off the microphone and camera on an Echo Spot or Echo Show

Push the microphone on/off button on the top of your Echo. The button shows a circle with a line through it. When the microphone is disabled, you'll see a red stripe running along the bottom of the display.

Manually cover the camera on an Echo Show

If you want to disable the camera on your Echo Show while leaving the microphone on, then push the slider button on the top of your Echo towards the right. This will slide a small piece of plastic in front of the camera lens, physically preventing anyone from seeing you through it.

Let Alexa guard your home

Alexa will listen for noises, turn on lights, and more...

With Alexa Guard, you can turn your Echo into an incredibly intelligent security device that can monitor your home while you're away. Here's a quick overview of each feature:

Emergency Helpline

With Alexa Guard Plus, you can say, *"Alexa, call for help"*, and your Echo will put you in touch with a trained agent who can request the dispatch of emergency responders — such as police, the fire department, or an ambulance.

Smart Alerts

If Alexa detects activity while you're away from home — like footsteps, a door closing, or glass breaking — she can send you a Smart Alert mobile notification and play a siren on your Echo. Alexa can also notify you about the sound of smoke alarms or carbon monoxide alarms.

Deter unwanted visitors

With Alexa Guard Plus, Alexa can turn on and off smart lights to make it look like someone is home, and if your smart camera detects motion outside, Alexa can play the sound of a dog barking from your Echo to help scare off potential intruders.

Only available in the US

At the time of writing, Alexa Guard is only available within the United States, but Amazon hopes to bring it to other countries soon.

Alexa Guard, or Alexa Guard Plus?

There are two types of Alexa Guard: the free version, which offers some helpful features for protecting your home, and a version called Alexa Guard Plus, which is priced $4.99 a month, or $49 a year. Here's a quick comparison between the two:

	Alexa Guard	Alexa Guard Plus
Call the Emergency Helpline from your Echo	✗	✓
Get Smart Alerts on your smartphone:		
Smoke & CO alarm sounds	✓	✓
Glass break sounds	✓	✓
Activity sounds	✗	✓
Deter unwanted visitors		
Auto turn on/off smart lights	✓	✓
Sound of dogs barking when motion is detected outside	✗	✓
Sound a siren when activity is detected inside	✗	✓

Find out more

To learn more about Alexa Guard, search the internet for "*Alexa guard*", then visit the first link.

Chapter 12

Troubleshooting

Alexa isn't perfect. If its connection to the internet is unreliable, then responses might take a while to arrive. You might find that a Bluetooth device has stopped connecting, or your Echo might become unresponsive. Thankfully these types of problems are very rare. Alexa is, in general, incredibly stable and reliable. Nevertheless, problems can arise, so this chapter takes a look at the most common troubleshooting problems and explains how you can fix them...

In this chapter:

Troubleshooting basics

A few suggestions to fix common problems...

It's more than frustrating when a piece of technology stops working. Something when using Alexa, you might find that commands are ignored or that Alexa just stops working entirely. Here are some things you can try when Alexa appears to be in a bad mood...

If Alexa doesn't understand what you're saying

Try standing closer to your Echo, and ensure there are no background noises like a TV.

If Alexa doesn't recognise you saying, "Alexa"...

Check to see if the Wake Word has been changed. The alternatives are "*Amazon*", "*Computer*", and "*Echo*".

To see what the current Wake Word is, open the Amazon Alexa app on your smartphone or tablet, tap **Devices**, select your Echo, then tap **WAKE WORD**. On the following screen, you'll see what the current choice is set to.

If Alexa isn't responding to voice commands...

Say "*Alexa, are you connected to the internet?*"

If it's not, try turning your router off and on again.

If Alexa is connected, make sure the microphone is enabled. If it's not, you'll see a solid red light ring running around your Echo, or a red bar running along the screen of your Echo Show. To turn the microphone back on, press the **microphone** button on top of your Echo.

If Alexa is taking ages to respond

Wait a few moments and try again. If the issue persists, turn off any Wi-Fi-connected devices you aren't using. For example, turn off Wi-Fi on your smartphone, computer, tablet, or even your smart TV. You can also try moving your Echo closer to the router, or try turning your router off and on again.

If you have restarted your router but Alexa is still not playing ball...

Restart your Echo device. To do this just unplug it from the wall and plug it back in. After a moment or two your Echo will be back up and running. Hopefully Alexa starts working again.

If Alexa is playing music on the wrong device

If you're asking Alexa to play music on an Echo device in one room, but it's actually playing in another, then chances are you have set up a smart home group, and the devices are not named correctly.

To find out which device has which name, open the Alexa app, tap **Devices**, choose **Echo & Alexa**, then look for the Echo device that you're trying to play music through. Once you've found it, make a mental note of the devices name, then say "*Alexa, play [song or album title] on [device name]*".

If Alexa is not streaming music

It's very likely that your internet connection is not running fast enough to stream audio. Try moving your Echo closer to the router, disconnecting any other Wi-Fi enabled devices, or restarting your router.

If you're convinced Alexa is not understanding you

Chances are it's not. You can take a look at your recent conversations with Alexa to see what it thought you said. If you said "*call Tom*", but Alexa heard, "*call Bob*", then it will show up in your voice history.

To see your voice history, open the Alexa app, tap **More**, choose **Settings**, then tap **Alexa Privacy**. On the following page, tap **Review Voice History**, then scroll through your recent interactions with Alexa to see what was heard.

If a specific skill isn't working

Ensure that your Echo is connected to Wi-Fi by saying, "*Alexa, are you connected to the internet?*" If it is, try disabling and then reenabling the skill. To do this say "*Alexa, disable [skill name]*", followed by, "*Alexa, enable [skill name]*".

Update your Echo

Make sure it's running the latest software...

Your Echo will try to keep itself up to date with the latest software from Amazon, so if things go as planned, you'll never know that an update has occurred. That being said, there might be rare occasions where an update is waiting for your confirmation. When that happens, the light ring will pulse blue, or you'll hear Alexa say, "An *update for this device is available*".

Force update an Echo Show or Spot

You can check for the latest software for your Echo Spot or Show by following these steps:

1. Swipe down from the top of the screen and select **Settings**.

2. Scroll down and select **Device Options**.

3. Tap **Check for Software Updates,** and your Echo will see that's available.

4. If an update is available, your Echo will automatically download and install it.

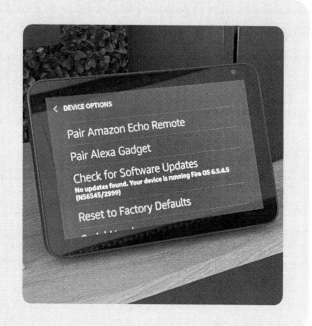

Check an Echo's software

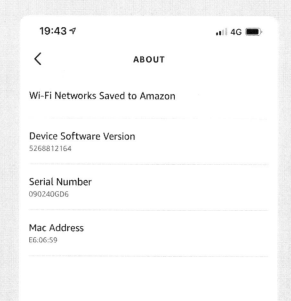

You can't force an Echo or Echo Dot to update, but you can see what software version it is current running. To find out:

1. Open the Amazon Alexa app on your smartphone or tablet, then tap **Devices**.

2. Tap on your Echo or Echo dot.

3. Scroll down, then tap **About**. On the following screen you will see the devices software version.

Make a note of the version number, then search the internet for "*amazon software update*". Click on the first link, then look for the latest software for your Echo. If the versions are different, make sure your Echo is connected to the internet. If if isn't, try resetting it or resetting your router.

Restart or reset your Echo

If nothing else works, try resetting your Echo...

The most common way to fix anything technical is to simply turn it off on then back on again. This works for desktop computers, smartphones, and even modern cars. If you've tried everything you can think of and Alexa is still refusing to work, then here's how to restart your Echo, or even restore it to its original state.

How to restart your Echo

Take a good look at your Echo, and you might notice something unusual: there's no on or off switch. Try asking Alexa to restart, and (perhaps rudely), it will just ignore you. The only way to restart your Echo is to unplug it from the wall, or if you have a power switch on the wall, flick it off. Wait a few seconds, then plug it back on. After a moment, your Echo will spring back into life as if nothing happened.

Factory reset your Echo

Think of factory resetting your Echo as the nuclear option. Maybe that's a little dramatic because while your Echo won't explode into a million pieces, it will return to the same factory status it was in when you first took it out of the box. It won't know who you are, what Wi-Fi connection to use, or be able to do anything useful at all. As a result, you'll need to go through the entire setup process all over again. You only need to factory reset your Echo if a) you're planning to give it to someone else, or b) everything else you've tried has failed to work.

Reset an Echo, Echo Dot

1. Press and hold the **Action** button for 25 seconds. The light ring will pulse orange, then turn off.

2. Wait for the light ring to turn back on and turn blue.

3. The light ring will then turn orange again, and the device enters the setup mode.

Reset an Echo Show/Studio

1. Press and hold the **Mute** and **Volume Down** buttons for about 15 seconds until you see the Amazon logo.

2. Follow the on-screen instructions to set up your Echo device once again.

Bluetooth problems

What to do if a Bluetooth device isn't communicating...

Alexa can interact with a wide number of Bluetooth devices, including headphones, speakers, and smartphones. In theory, connecting via Bluetooth should easy, but spotty connections and device compatibility issues can often get in the way. Here are some helpful tips for those irksome situations...

If Alexa can't see a Bluetooth device

Sometimes you can ask Alexa to connect to a Bluetooth device and nothing will happen. When this happens, try the following:

- The first step is to make sure the Bluetooth device is turned on and fully charged.

- Make sure the Bluetooth device is within 33 feet of your Echo. Keep in mind that thick walls can reduce this distance.

- Ensure the Bluetooth device is in pairing mode. Many Bluetooth devices have a specific button for this. If not, try using its setting screen to enable pairing.

With these steps completed:

- If you have an Echo Spot or Show, swipe down from the top of the screen, tap **Settings**, then choose **Bluetooth**. If you see the device you're trying to connect to, tap on it.

- For Echo devices without a screen, open the Alexa app, tap **Devices**, select your Echo, then tap **Speaker**. On the following screen, tap **Bluetooth**, tap **NEXT**, then look for your Bluetooth device.

If a Bluetooth device requires a PIN

Many Bluetooth devices require you to enter a six-digit PIN number before they can connect. Unfortunately, at the time of writing Alexa devices don't support this feature. They can only connect to Bluetooth devices with no PIN requirements.

Alexa misunderstanding

What to do if Alexa is constantly misunderstanding you...

It's worth noting that Alexa's voice recognition is perhaps the best in the world. Not only can it hear you over background noises, but it can also hear you at a distance and even distinguish between multiple voices in a household. That being said, Alexa isn't perfect, so you're very likely to encounter situations when Alexa mishears you, sometimes repeatedly. If that's happening to you, then here are a few things you can try:

- Stand closer to your Echo. Yes, this is a simple "fix", but if you're standing too far away, Alexa might mishear words.

- Make sure nothing is covering or blocking the Echo's microphone. Ideally, it should be on a hard surface, in plain view of the room.

- Move your Echo away from walls or corners. Hard surfaces can often cause reverberations that affect sound clarity.

- Restart your Echo. To do this just turn it off at the power source, then turn it back on.

- Turn down the volume of media. If your Echo is playing a loud music track or video, the outputting sound might interfere with the microphone's ability to listen to you.

- Check to see what Alexa heard. If you said "*call Tom*", but Alexa heard, "*call Bob*", then it will show up in your voice history. To see your voice history, open the Alexa app, tap **More**, choose **Settings**, then tap **Alexa Privacy**. On the following page, tap **Review Voice History**, then scroll through your recent interactions with Alexa to see what was heard.

Ask Alexa to learn your voice

We covered this at the start of the book, but if you haven't set it up yet, then asking Alexa to recognise your voice is one of the best ways to ensure Alexa can understand what you're stating.

When you're ready to ask Alexa to learn your voice, first make sure that there are no background noises and that only once Echo device is within earshot. Next, say, "*Alexa, learn my voice*". Alexa will then greet you and you to repeat a few sentences, such as, "*Alexa, search for holiday music*". Once your voice has been recognised, you can get other household members to repeat the process.

Phone call problems

Solutions for phone and video calls not going through...

Making video and phone calls through your Echo is one of the more unique features that Alexa can perform, but calls don't always go perfectly. If you're having problems making a call, then here are some suggestions you can try:

- If you've asked Alexa to call a number, but it's not working, double-check that you're stating the correct number. Alexa might be trying to call a non-existent line, or even a stranger.

- If you're asking Alexa to call someone in your contacts, but it can't find the person, make sure you're using the correct name or nickname. If you've just made a change to the contacts list on your phone, then wait a while for the update to go through to Alexa.

- If Alexa isn't making landline calls, make sure you're within the United States. This feature will not work outside of the USA.

- If you're trying to call the emergency services, then keep in mind that Alexa won't make 911/999 calls. Grab your smartphone if you're in an emergency.

- Check your voice history to see what Alexa heard. To do this open the Alexa app, tap **More**, choose **Settings**, then tap **Alexa Privacy**. On the following page, tap **Review Voice History**.

- Make sure your Echo is connected to the internet. To check, say out loud, "*Alexa, are you connected to the internet?*"

- If Alexa isn't connected to the internet, try restarting your router. If that still doesn't help, make sure the router isn't near devices that can cause interference, such as microwave ovens and large electronic devices.

If you can't place an order

What to do if Alexa won't purchase items from Amazon...

With literally millions of items, eBooks, games, and things to buy on Amazon, it only makes sense that it's very own digital assistant can suggest and purchase items from the Amazon website. If Alexa is refusing to make a purchase, then here are some helpful tips:

- Make sure that your Amazon account has a valid payment method, and that your personal information is up to date. To check, head over to the Amazon website on your computer or the Amazon app on your smartphone, visit the **Your Account** area, and make sure everything is correct.

- If you use a 4-digit voice code to confirm your purchases, make sure you're using the right code.

Confirm Voice Purchasing is enabled

To do this, open the Amazon Alexa app and then:

1. Tap **More**, then choose **Settings**.
2. Tap **Account Settings**, then choose **Voice Purchasing**.
3. Ensure the **Voice Purchasing** toggle switch is turned on.

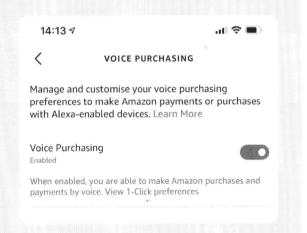

Make sure you're Voice Profile is enabled

If you use voice profiles for purchases, make sure that your voice profile is enabled to place orders. To do this:

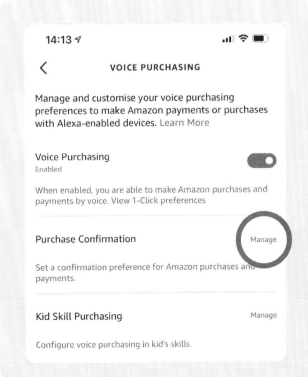

1. Open the Amazon Alexa app on your smartphone or tablet, tap **More**, then choose **Settings**.
2. Tap **Account Settings**, then choose **Voice Purchasing**.
3. Tap **Purchase Confirmation**.
4. Tap **Manage**, then select **Voice Profile**.
5. On the following screen, turn a **Saved Profile** on or off.

Update a Wi-Fi password

Tell your Echo that you've updated the Wi-Fi password..

It's a good idea to regularly update your Wi-Fi password, especially if you live in a busy neighbourhood or have lots of visitors to your home or workplace. By doing this, you can prevent anyone from abusing your Wi-Fi signal, or perhaps, more importantly, your bandwidth allocation.

There's a pretty big downside to updating your Wi-Fi password: you'll need to update every device connected to your Wi-Fi to tell them of the change. Here's how to tell your Echo that the password has changed:

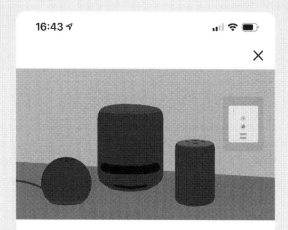

Is your Echo Dot plugged in and displaying an orange light?

Update the password using the Alexa app

If you have an Echo Dot, Echo Studio, or another Echo device without a touchscreen...

1 Open the Amazon Alexa app on your smartphone or tablet, tap **Devices**, then choose your Echo.

2 Where it says Wi-Fi Network, tap the **Change** link to its right.

3 Follow the on-screen instructions to reconnect your Echo to Wi-Fi.

Update the password on an Echo Show

If you have an Echo device with a touchscreen, then here's how to quickly update the Wi-Fi password:

1 Swipe down from the top of the screen, then tap **Settings**.

2 Tap **Network**. Look for your Wi-Fi network, then tap the info icon to the right of it.

3 Tap **Forget**. Your Echo will then disconnect from your Wi-Fi and return to the list of available networks.

4 Tap on your Wi-Fi network once again, then enter the new password. If prompted, enter the password used for your Amazon account.

Smart-home device not working

If a plug, light, or camera is not connecting...

There are countless smart devices available for Alexa, including smart lights, baby monitors, plugs, security cameras, door locks... you name it. When one of them stops working with Alexa, then here are a few suggestions:

- First of all, make sure the smart device is powered on or plugged in. If the smart device requires batteries, make sure they haven't run out.

- Try turning the smart device on and off. If it doesn't have an on/off switch, try unplugging it from the power source. Often this is the simplest way to get a device to start working again.

- If the smart device communicates over Wi-Fi, make sure it's connected and using the correct password. If everything seems correct, try restarting your own router.

- If the smart device requires an app to work, make sure you've installed it and set it up. Often smart devices will require you to sign in to an account or use a subscription, and these are nearly always managed via an app.

- If the smart device you have requires an Alexa skill, try disabling the skill and then re-enabling it.

- Update the smart device's software or firmware. You can usually do this via an app related to the smart device.

- Make sure both the smart device and Wi-Fi router are free of anything that might cause interference. Also, keep in mind that many Bluetooth smart devices can only communicate within a short distance.

Index A-S

Quickly find what you're looking for...

Index S-V

Quickly find what you're looking for...

Stay inspired

Seniors Guides:

Seniors Guide to iPad

978-1-914347-01-6
$19.75 USA
$22.99 CAN
£10.99 UK
$22.99 AUD

Seniors Guide to MacBook

978-1-914347-02-3
$19.75 USA
$22.99 CAN
£10.99 UK
$22.99 AUD

Seniors Guide to iPhone

978-1-914347-00-9
$19.75 USA
$22.99 CAN
£10.99 UK
$22.99 AUD

Beginners Guides:

iPad Manual For Beginners

978-1-914347-98-6
$19.75 USA
$22.99 CAN
£10.99 UK
$22.99 AUD

MacBook Manual For Beginners

978-1-914347-99-3
$19.75 USA
$22.99 CAN
£10.99 UK
$22.99 AUD

Other Guides:

iPhone 12 Guide

979-8699016419
$12.98 USA
$14.98 CAN
£9.98 UK

iPad Pro Guide

979-8651084746
$12.98 USA
$14.98 CAN
£9.98 UK

iMac Guide

979-8699016419
$12.98 USA
$14.98 CAN
£9.98 UK

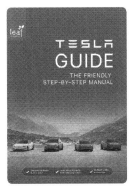

Tesla Guide

979-8651084746
$12.98 USA
$14.98 CAN
£9.98 UK

Tesla Model 3 Guide

979-8651084746
$12.98 USA
$14.98 CAN
£9.98 UK

Visit www.leafpublishing.co.uk to find out more

Made in United States
Orlando, FL
03 November 2021

RECEIVED NOV -- 2021